Volume 2

ARCHES

BONE STRUCTURE

GROWING UP WITH SCIENCE

AN ALPHABETIC ENCYCLOPEDIA THAT ANSWERS
FOR YOUNGER READERS THE "HOWS," "WHATS" and "WHYS"
OF THE SCIENTIFIC WORLD IN WHICH THEY LIVE
AMONG SUBJECTS DISCUSSED IN THIS VOLUME ARE:

- Astronomy
- Atoms and Molecules
- Automobiles
- Avionics
- Balloons
- Barometers
- Bathyscaphe
- Bells
- Biorythms

GROWING UP WITH SCIENCE

THE ILLUSTRATED ENCYCLOPEDIA OF
INVENTION

VOLUME
2

H. S. STUTTMAN, INC. *publishers*   Westport, Connecticut 06889

Library of Congress Cataloging in Publication Data
Main entry under title:

Growing up with science.

  Includes index.
  Summary: A twenty-five-volume, alphabetically-arranged
science encyclopedia.
  1. Science—Dictionaries, Juvenile. 2. Technology—
Dictionaries, Juvenile. 3. Inventions—Dictionaries,
Juvenile. [1. Science—Dictionaries] I. Dempsey,
Michael W. II. Paton, John, 1914-   III. Wicks,
Keith. IV. Evans, Humphrey.
Q121.G764 1984   503'.21   82-63047
ISBN 0-87475-830-0 (v. 1)

Published by H. S. STUTTMAN INC.
Westport, Connecticut 06889
© Marshall Cavendish Limited 1984

Arches

Almost everything that is built to take great pressure is curved—from the hull of a submarine to a high concrete dam. Rounded objects can take more pressure than ones with straight sides and corners. This is why arches have been used since ancient times to support buildings.

An arch is a structure that is built to cover an opening, such as a door or a window, and support weight above it. The arch is stronger than a simple flat beam across the top of an opening. The stones in the middle of the arch do not fall because they are wedge-shaped. They are pushed down by the weight on top of them, but this downward push presses them out against the stones next to them. So the main push is sideways, instead of downward.

Each stone helps to support every other stone in an arch. As long as the side supports of the door or window stay upright, the arch above them will not fall. But if the doorway sides were pushed outward, the arch would collapse. In big buildings, such as cathedrals, large arches produce so much outward pressure that the side supports are often held up by heavy masses of stone called BUTTRESSES.

The parts of an arch

When a stone arch is built it is usually supported by a wooden framework until the center stone at the top is dropped into place. This center stone is called the keystone because, when it is in position, it locks the whole arch together.

The other main parts of an arch are the voussoirs, the imposts and the span. The voussoirs are the wedge-shaped blocks which make up the arch. The keystone is larger than the voussoirs, and is often decorated. Imposts are the points on either side of the arch from

Below left: The main parts of an arch. The keystone is the important center block that holds the whole arch together. The rise is the height of the arch. This type of arch is called semicircular. The small drawing shows how an arch turns the downward pressure of the wall above it into an outward thrust.

Below right: Some of the many types of arches. The first two in the top row are not true arches at all. They push straight down instead of spreading the weight sideways. The next one, the triangular arch, is a real arch in spite of its shape. Sometimes the arch is made of a single piece of concrete. The parabolic arch is like this.

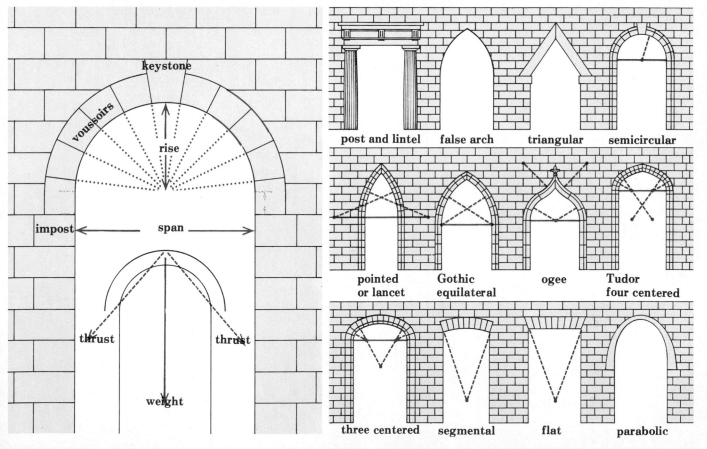

keystone
voussoirs
rise
impost
span
thrust   thrust
weight

post and lintel   false arch   triangular   semicircular

pointed or lancet   Gothic equilateral   ogee   Tudor four centered

three centered   segmental   flat   parabolic

which the arch rises. The span is the space between the side supports.

The history of the arch

Arches were first made by the ancient Assyrians and Babylonians. The Egyptians used them too, but it was the Romans who first began to use arches in many of their buildings. Triumphal arches, bridges and aqueducts (bridges for carrying water over valleys) still stand to remind us of the skill of these early Roman builders.

Triumphal arches were also built at a much later date, and many of them are copies of early Roman arches. Examples of these are the Arc de Triomphe in Paris and Marble Arch in London. Probably the best known arch in the United States is the huge Gateway Arch at St. Louis, Missouri. It is 630 feet (192 meters) high, shaped like a perfect PARABOLA and is made of steel in a concrete base.

Different kinds of arches

Different periods of history, and different parts of the world, have produced arches of many shapes and sizes. The classical arch was semicircular. In this type, half the distance between the imposts (the side supports) equalled the height of the rise (see diagram on the previous page). Later, in the Gothic period of architecture, arches became taller and more pointed. The ogee arch came to a sharp point at the top. The Tudor, or "four-centered," arch had flattened middle sections and sharper curves at the sides. It was stronger than the earlier arches.

Most arches built today are to be found in bridges. With today's materials of steel and concrete, very large spans can be built. The longest arch bridge in the world is the New River Gorge bridge near Fayetteville, West Virginia. It has a span of 1700 feet (518 meters).

See also: **BRIDGES,
BUILDING TECHNIQUES**

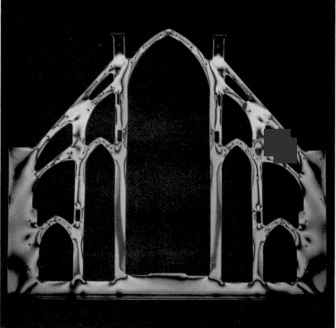

Right above: The Romans were the first great arch builders. They used the arch for aqueducts, bridges and triumphal monuments. This picture shows the Roman aqueduct at Segovia in Spain. It was built around 100 AD.

Right below: A plastic model of the arches of a French cathedral. This model is used to show the stresses in the real building. The distortion is shown up by special photography. Although this type of building looks light and fragile, it is really very strong because of the arches.

Artificial Limbs and Joints

Artificial limbs are used to replace limbs that have been removed by surgery because of injury, infection or poor blood supply. Today's artificial limbs give people the chance to move around and enjoy an active life.

When someone loses an arm or a leg nowadays, doctors and engineers can give the patient a new artificial limb that looks and works very much like the lost one. New, strong, light alloys and plastics have helped people who design artificial limbs to improve both the working and appearance of the limbs. They can also use special hard-wearing, low-friction hinges and joints with electronic controls.

Artificial legs

Artificial limbs can be divided into two kinds—unpowered and powered. Unpowered limbs rely on the movements of the patient's body for their control.

For artificial legs, unpowered limbs are usually still used. A person's legs must support the weight of the whole body, and allow him or her to move about easily. The place where the leg has been amputated is, of course, very important. The more of the limb that is left, the more control he or she will have over the artificial limb.

Most artificial legs are held in place by a combination of straps and a slight suction effect caused by the damaged leg sitting in a cup at the top of the artificial limb. The wearer soon learns to control the leg.

The design of the ankle and knee joints can be quite complicated. At the heel and instep, rubber bumpers are used to ABSORB the impact as the heel touches the ground and to allow a smooth "rollover" during walking. Knee joints usually have devices which allow the patient to walk at different speeds while keeping up a normal looking step.

Each artificial limb is put together specially for the patient.

Hands and arms

Artificial hands are more difficult to make than legs. Our hands are so complicated and clever, it is impossible to make artificial ones that are as good. There is, however, a great deal of research going on to improve artificial hands and arms.

Some limbs have been designed which can be

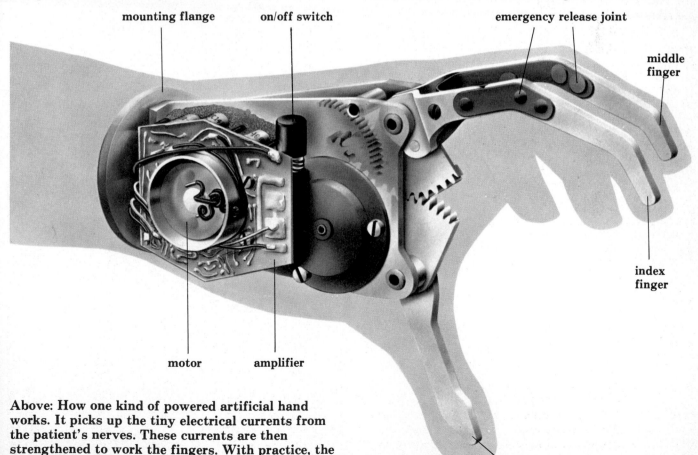

mounting flange   on/off switch   emergency release joint   middle finger   index finger   motor   amplifier   thumb

Above: How one kind of powered artificial hand works. It picks up the tiny electrical currents from the patient's nerves. These currents are then strengthened to work the fingers. With practice, the user can move that hand just by willing it to move.

attached to the patient's existing muscles in such a way that movement of the artificial hand is actually controlled by the patient's brain.

Brain signals

Our muscles are controlled by electrical signals from the brain. The brain can still send out signals, even when the limb is no longer there. In one type of artificial hand, small electrical signals from the brain are picked up by nerve-endings in the muscle that remains. These tiny signals are magnified and used to control the artificial hand. The patient "thinks" the artificial hand to act in a certain way. After some practice he or she can manage even quite delicate operations.

Artificial arms of this kind can be powered by compressed gas or by electric motors.

When the patient has lost an arm above the elbow, a special system of straps and cables is often used. The patient is trained to make movements of the shoulder, the back and the arm stump. These movements, by means of the straps and cables, allow him or her to lock and unlock the artificial elbow joint, move the forearm up and down and work the hand.

Power for the arm or leg

Controlling an artificial limb is usually more difficult than powering it. But new ideas for both are always

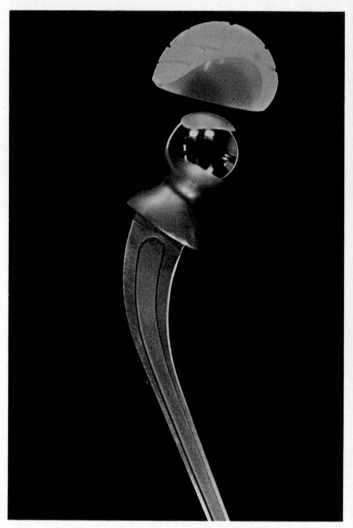

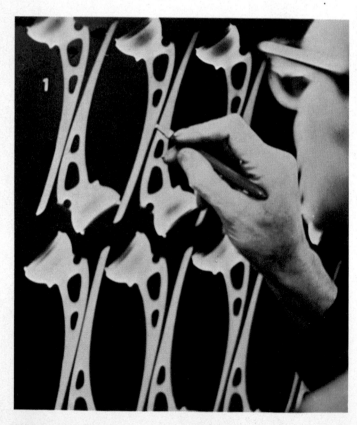

Above: A complete artificial hip joint. The socket that is attached to the hip bone is made of polyethylene plastic. The ball that moves in this socket is highly polished steel—so highly polished that the photographer and his lights are seen reflected in it. Attached to the ball is the stem which is cemented into the patient's thigh bone with special acrylic adhesive.

Left: The steel used for many hip joints is called vitallium. This is an alloy of cobalt, chromium and molybdenum, with small amounts of other materials. This metal is so hard it cannot be smoothed by machining. The steel ball and its stem have to be cast in the correct shape. This can cause problems because the slightest flaw in the metal makes it useless. The picture shows X-rays of hip joint castings being carefully examined to detect the smallest flaw.

appearing. The heel pump and the use of ELECTRO-HYDRAULIC systems are modern power methods. The electrohydraulic system has a container with liquid under pressure in it. This pressure is kept up by an electric pump worked from batteries.

In the case of the heel pump, the pressure in the container is kept up by a small pump built into the heel of the patient's shoe. When he or she walks, liquid is forced up a tube to maintain the pressure in the container. It is the pressure of the liquid in the container that the patient uses to move the artificial limb when he or she wants to.

Artificial joints

One of the most common operations, and one of the most successful, is that for replacing the hip joint. This operation becomes necessary when arthritis or inflammation of the joint begins to cause the patient severe pain. A patient who has a new hip joint is often changed from being an invalid to being an active person once more.

The materials used for the new joint must not be rejected by the patient's body, and they must not wear out over the years. After many years of research, it was found that the best materials for the artificial joint are a very smooth metal ball that fits into a plastic cup-shaped socket. These two parts of the joint are fixed to the thigh bone and the hip bone by special cement. There is a picture of the parts on the previous page. Once fitted, these joints should last for at least 30 years.

There are also operations to replace the knee joint, elbow joint and the small joints in the fingers.

A small number of patients are allergic to artificial joints. Their bodies try to reject the tiny particles of plastic and metal that are produced by the friction (rubbing) of the joint. Patients are usually tested before the operation to find out whether or not they are allergic to the materials to be used.

The plastic adhesives used to cement the artificial joints in position sometimes cause trouble, too. One of the main difficulties is cementing the metal to the bone. Special acrylic adhesive is used for this.

The future

There is no doubt that in the field of artificial limbs there will be tremendous advances in the years to come. New materials which are stronger and lighter than those used at present are already being tested. Electronics and the SILICON CHIP will certainly play a big part in helping those who have been unfortunate enough to lose a limb. The science of artificial limbs has come a very long way from Captain Hook's crude iron claw in *Peter Pan*.

See also: ALLERGY, BONE STRUCTURE, BRAIN

Below: A modern artificial leg is made to match the appearance of the other (real) leg as closely as possible. This is done by photographing the good leg in a special way so that the shapes of the leg show up. These photographs can then be scanned by a computer which stores the exact shape of the leg in its memory. The computer is then made to control the machine that shapes the artificial leg so that it exactly matches the real leg.

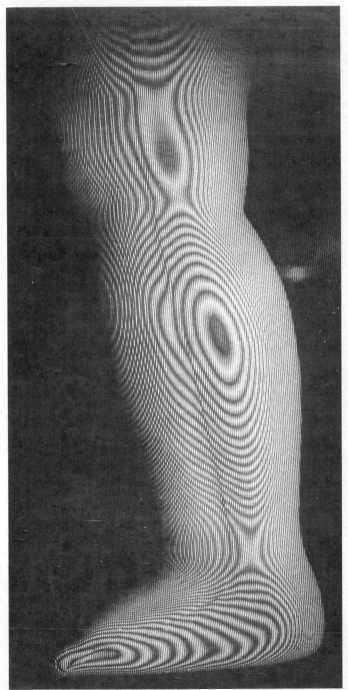

Asbestos

Asbestos is a material which does not melt or catch fire when it is put into flames. It also helps to hold off heat because heat goes through it very slowly. Workers have to be careful how they handle asbestos, however, because it can cause lung disease.

There are several types of asbestos. They are all minerals that can be found in rocks. The rock is mined and then passed through a series of crushers and rollers to separate the fibers of asbestos from the crushed rock. These fibers are spun and woven or pressed together to make asbestos cloth. Heat-resistant articles such as automobile brake linings, fireproof suits, theater safety curtains and INSULATION for electric cables are all made from asbestos. Asbestos also does not allow electricity to pass through it, which is why it is used for electric cables.

Fire-resistant asbestos cement sheets are made by mixing cement and asbestos fibers in water. Some pipes are also made from asbestos cement.

Other uses for this important mineral are in the production of reinforced plastics and for storage containers in the chemical industry. It has also been used in rocket heat-shields.

Asbestos production

Most of the world's asbestos is mined in the Quebec region of Canada and the Ural Mountains of Russia. It is often necessary to crush 100 tons of rock to get 5 tons of asbestos.

Above: Testing a flameproof suit made with asbestos. Asbestos is an ideal material for protective clothing. It is fire resistant and heat goes through it very slowly. Flameproof clothing often has a silvery outer surface to deflect as much heat as possible.

Below: Workers who deal with asbestos have to wear protective clothing and masks.

Did you know?

The heat resistance of asbestos has been known for many hundreds of years. King Charlemagne of France even had a tablecloth made of asbestos. When it became stained, it was just thrown in the fire to clean it, then pulled out and used again.

The dangers of asbestos

When asbestos is being manufactured, the air is often filled with tiny fibers of the material. In the past, these fibers were breathed in by the workers and many of them fell ill with lung disease.

The disease caused by breathing in asbestos dust is called asbestosis. A patient with this disease becomes very short of breath. Unfortunately, asbestos fibers can also cause cancer—especially cancer of the lung.

The dangers of breathing in asbestos are, however, now well-known and workers are protected by federal and state regulations. They must wear masks and protective clothing and have regular medical checks.

Assembly Line

An assembly line is a team of people working together to produce a finished item. Factories making automobiles, televisions and typewriters all have assembly lines. It is an effective way of making products quickly and cheaply.

It was Henry Ford who first introduced the assembly line into his factory for making the famous Model T. Other manufacturers were using the accepted way of making automobiles. Men worked in groups on one automobile until it was finished. Ford saw that this way was inefficient. It was better to train a worker to do one small job really fast, rather than let him do hundreds of tasks at his own pace.

Ford controlled the speed of each small job by keeping the partly made car moving down a long factory building. As it passed each worker he had just time to do his task before the next partly made car arrived. He did not have to leave his "station" to fetch the part he had to bolt onto the car. It was brought to him on a conveyor belt.

At one end of the assembly line the first few parts were brought together. At the other end of the same line completely finished cars were rolled away ready for the final polish and inspection. In between were cars in all the stages of manufacture.

Saving time and money

Speeding up the work meant that more cars were produced in a week by the same number of workers. This reduced the cost of each car.

But there were other savings, too. Ford was able to forecast much more accurately how many cars would be built in a week. This meant that he could buy materials and parts only when they were really needed.

Other manufacturers saw the advantages of Ford's methods, and it was not long before the assembly line spread not only to the rest of the auto industry, but to other similar industries, too. Nowadays few products are made by the old methods.

But workers often find assembly work boring, and

Below: Assembly line work in the aircraft industry. Many of the parts are made in other factories.

some companies are trying modern versions of group working again to keep their workers happy.

Modern assembly lines

Automobiles are one of the most complicated assembly jobs in modern manufacture. The thousands of parts are made by dozens of different manufacturers. Steering columns, back axles, instruments, lights, radiators, are all taken into the stores from different suppliers until it is time for them to be fitted to their cars.

Very careful planning is needed to make sure that all the parts are in the right place on the assembly line. And there must be enough of each part to keep the assembly line running without a break. As many as 1500 cars a week can be made on one assembly line. One missing part can stop the whole line.

In actual fact, cars are made on two lines running one beside the other. One carries the "working" parts—the engine, transmission, wheels and brakes. The other takes the bodywork which needs different treatment—for example, spraying with paint. At a point on the assembly lines where both are ready, the body and the transmission systems are put together and continue down a single line from then on. It is on this final line that the fuel tank, lights, instruments and steering column are added, together with the seats and other fittings inside the car.

The last part of the assembly line is where the cars are tested. This is done on a "rolling road," a set of rollers, so that the engine and transmission can be tested on a car while it is standing still.

Other assembly lines

Even such large items as airplanes are made on an assembly line. The body (fuselage) is assembled first. Then the wings and tail are added, followed by the engines, controls and instruments. These are almost always made by other manufacturers and just bolted in place. The whole airframe is moved along an assembly line as each part is added.

Electronic devices, such as radios, televisions and computers, would be impossible to make so cheaply without assembly lines. The separate components are often still inserted by hand into the circuit boards, but sometimes this is now done by machines. Soldering (joining metal surfaces with melted metal alloy) is done by passing the assembled circuit board across a bath of solder. The solder sticks only to the connections on the circuit board: everywhere else it is repelled.

Introducing robots

Assembly lines are ideally suited for automation. Electric light bulbs were among the first to be made entirely by machine. The glass bulbs are formed, the filament added, the bulb filled with gas and sealed, all by machine, quickly and without any waste. Robots are

now even making such complex items as automobiles.

See also: **BATTERY AND INTENSIVE FARMING, PRINTED CIRCUIT, ROBOTS**

Below: An assembly line in a television factory. The shell of the television joins the line at the far end and parts are added by each operator.

Right: Automobile assembly lines vary from factory to factory. The complete engine is always built up on a separate assembly line from the body. At a carefully chosen point in the line, the body meets up with the engine and transmission. Then the interior trim, radiator, hydraulic and fuel systems are added. Last of all the seats and wheels are fitted.

Below: Part of an assembly line for electric typewriters. The typewriters travel along a roller conveyor on trays. Each operator takes a typewriter from the conveyor, adds a part and puts the machine back on the conveyor. It then moves along to the next operator.

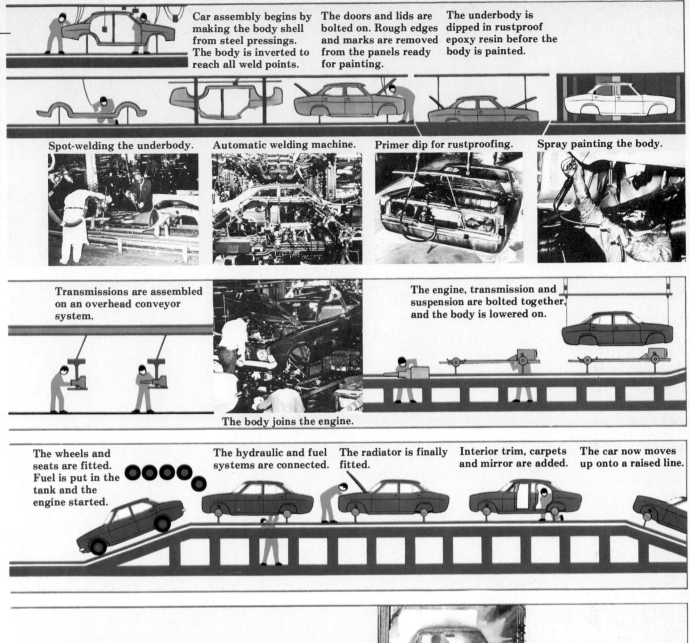

Car assembly begins by making the body shell from steel pressings. The body is inverted to reach all weld points.

The doors and lids are bolted on. Rough edges and marks are removed from the panels ready for painting.

The underbody is dipped in rustproof epoxy resin before the body is painted.

Spot-welding the underbody.

Automatic welding machine.

Primer dip for rustproofing.

Spray painting the body.

Transmissions are assembled on an overhead conveyor system.

The engine, transmission and suspension are bolted together, and the body is lowered on.

The body joins the engine.

The wheels and seats are fitted. Fuel is put in the tank and the engine started.

The hydraulic and fuel systems are connected.

The radiator is finally fitted.

Interior trim, carpets and mirror are added.

The car now moves up onto a raised line.

The finished car is driven up on a ramp where the steering and suspension are adjusted and checked. The car is then driven onto the test rollers.

On the rollers, the engine, transmission, steering, brakes and lights are checked. After a road test the car is sprayed to test for any leaks.

A car being spray-tested.

Astronomical Telescope

Telescopes are the most important of the astronomer's instruments. Today, astronomers use powerful telescopes that let us see objects so far away that their light has been traveling toward us since the universe began about 15 thousand million years ago.

The Italian astronomer Galileo first pointed a telescope at the night sky in 1609. He could see four moons of the planet Jupiter and the mountains of the moon. His simple telescope used glass lenses to collect and focus the light.

Collecting light
Astronomers want to observe faraway objects, so the telescopes they use are made to collect as much light as possible. The larger the opening—the APERTURE—of a telescope, the brighter the star appears. The iris of our eye can open no wider than about 0.3 inch (8 millimeters). There are huge telescopes with apertures of over 200 inches (5 meters) which can collect several million times as much light as the eye.

Different types of telescope
There are two ways in which telescopes collect and focus light. The first is by REFRACTION (using a lens); the other is by REFLECTION (using a mirror). The size of the lens or mirror determines the amount of light the telescope collects. The amount of light collected controls how much detail can be seen. Today, most big telescopes are reflectors. Refractors were more common a hundred years ago.

Refracting telescopes
The refracting telescope uses a glass lens (object glass) to focus the light—that is to bring it to a sharp image at the bottom of the telescope tube. There, the astronomer can look at the image through an eyepiece which is usually no more than a simple magnifying glass.

The distance between the object glass and the image is called the FOCAL LENGTH. If we divide the focal length by the DIAMETER of the opening we get a number called the focal ratio. A 2-inch lens with a focal length of 30 inches has a focal ratio of 15 (30÷2). This is written f15.

The magnification (how much bigger something looks) of any telescope depends on the eyepiece. Like the object glass, the eyepiece has its own focal length. The magnification of a telescope is given by the focal length of the object glass divided by the focal length of the eyepiece.

A disadvantage of the refractor is the difficulty in making large lenses that are free from blemishes in the glass. And the lens shape—thick in the middle and thin at the edge—means that the thick center piece has to be supported by the thin edge piece. This causes the lens

to sag very slightly. But if the lens is made thicker, to give more strength, the glass ABSORBS some of the light passing through it and cancels out the advantage of the larger opening.

The largest refractor in the world is at Yerkes Observatory, Wisconsin. It has an aperture of 40 inches (101 centimeters) and a focal length of 62 feet (18.6 meters). This telescope was built in 1897.

Reflecting telescopes
Astronomers are specially interested in faraway objects in the sky. They, therefore, need telescopes that collect as much light as possible. The reflecting telescope does this job well. It can be smaller than the refracting telescope, and large mirrors can be made strong enough to stop them distorting. Unlike a lens, a

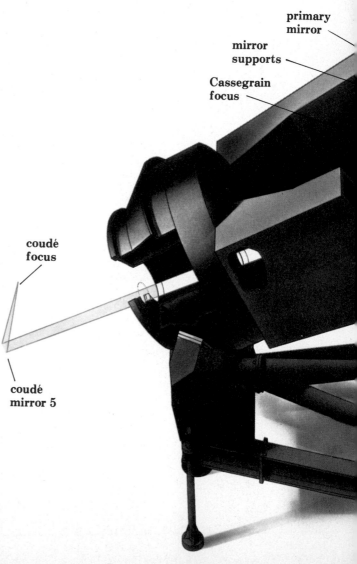

primary mirror

mirror supports

Cassegrain focus

coudé focus

coudé mirror 5

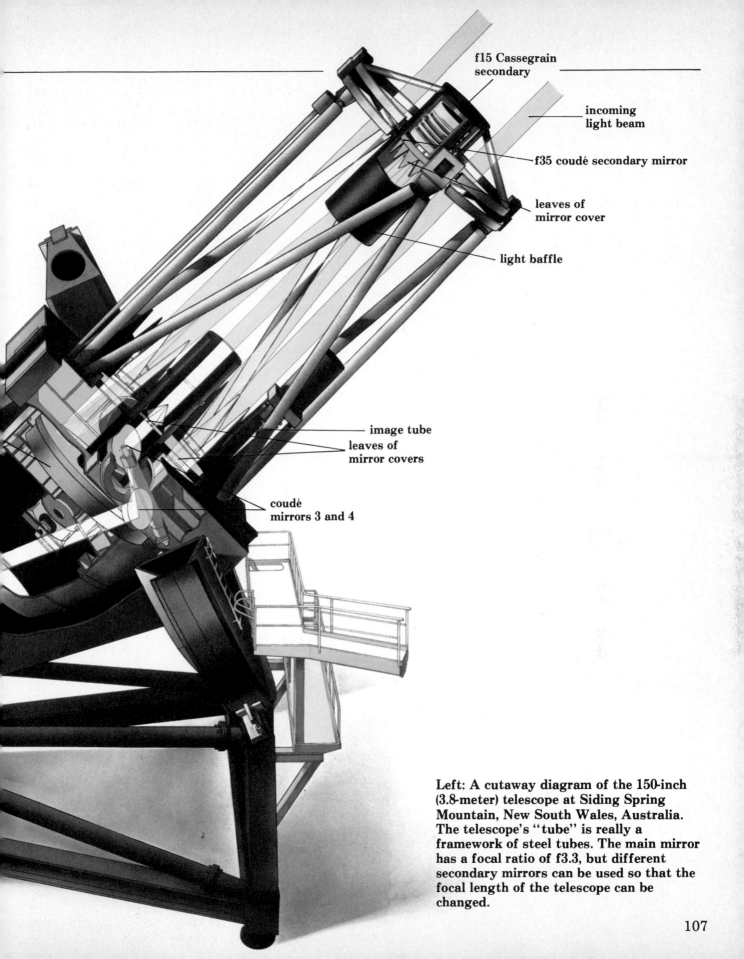

f15 Cassegrain secondary

incoming light beam

f35 coudé secondary mirror

leaves of mirror cover

light baffle

image tube

leaves of mirror covers

coudé mirrors 3 and 4

Left: A cutaway diagram of the 150-inch (3.8-meter) telescope at Siding Spring Mountain, New South Wales, Australia. The telescope's "tube" is really a framework of steel tubes. The main mirror has a focal ratio of f3.3, but different secondary mirrors can be used so that the focal length of the telescope can be changed.

mirror can be supported over the whole of its back surface. The largest telescopes in the world are reflectors.

The reflecting telescope uses a big concave (saucer-shaped) mirror to gather light. This mirror is usually made from glass, coated with a shining layer of silver or aluminum. Unlike a normal mirror, in which the back of the glass is coated with a reflecting layer of silver, a telescope mirror is coated on its front surface.

There are several kinds of reflecting telescope. The simplest, and the most popular with amateur astronomers, is the Newtonian telescope. It is called this because it was designed by the great English scientist Isaac Newton in the 16th century. The main (primary) mirror is at the bottom of the telescope tube. Light entering the tube strikes the mirror and is reflected back to a focus near the top end. Before it comes to a focus, however, it is reflected out through a hole in the side of the tube by a small flat mirror, called a secondary mirror. This arrangement allows the eyepiece to be placed where the observer's head does not get in the way of the light.

The big reflectors

To get a longer focal length and, therefore, more magnification, a convex secondary mirror is made to reflect the light back down the tube instead of pushing it out at the side (see diagram). This reflects the light back in a narrow cone and increases the focal length by four or five times, without increasing the length of the tube.

A small hole is cut in the center of the main mirror so that the light can be brought to a focus just behind it. This type of telescope is called *Cassegrain*, and it is this kind of instrument that is used by professional astronomers. Their telescopes often have two or three different secondary mirrors to give different focal lengths.

In another type of reflecting telescope, called the *Coudé* system, the light is reflected by a number of mirrors through the telescope mounting into a separate room. Delicate apparatus can be kept here at a special temperature in a controlled clean area. This type of telescope is used for analyzing the light from stars to find out what chemicals the stars are made of.

One disadvantage of ordinary telescopes is that only a very small area of the sky can be seen at a time. To overcome this, in 1930 Bernhard Schmidt invented a new kind of telescope with a special set of lenses. It gave a wide-angle view of the sky. Today astronomers use the Schmidt telescope before focusing on selected objects with their big reflectors.

The giants

For many years the world's largest reflecting telescope was the 200-inch (5-meter) giant at Mount Palomar in California. It is housed in a dome 140 feet (42 meters) across and can be pointed at any part of the sky. This

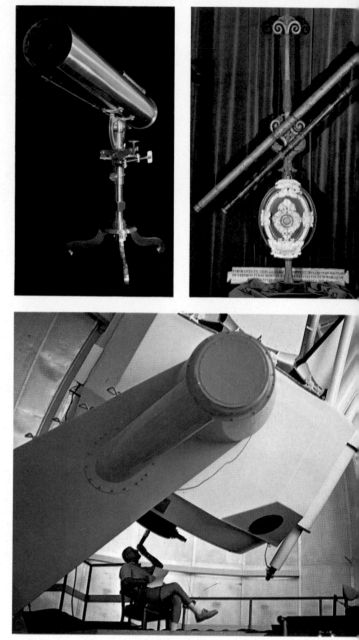

Above: An astronomer using the 84-inch (2.1-meter) reflecting telescope at Kitt Peak, Arizona. Astronomers do not often look directly through big telescopes like this. The small telescope attached at the right is used for finding the right part of the sky before using the main instrument.

Top right: Galileo's original telescope, now in a museum in Florence, Italy.

Top left: An 18th century reflecting telescope. It is similar to a modern *Cassegrain* type.

telescope has been very successful in probing deeper into space.

Even the Palomar giant was outdone when a 236-inch (6-meter) reflector was built at Zelenchukskaya in Russia. An instrument like this can pick up stars 16 million times fainter than the faintest star that can be seen with the naked eye.

Photographing the sky

Today's astronomers spend little time actually looking through telescopes. Instead, they use the camera. The photographic plate can be used to collect light over long periods of time. This makes it possible to locate objects which cannot be seen by looking through the telescope. Photographic exposures may last for several hours.

While the photograph is being taken, the earth is spinning on its axis. This means that the star "moves." So the telescope must be guided to follow the star. This is done by very accurate machinery which drives the telescope at exactly the right speed to counteract the effect of the earth's spin.

Electronic devices are now attached to telescopes to boost the faint light from faraway stars.

Telescopes of the future

For a long time astronomical telescopes have been built in places which are high and well away from cities. But all earth-bound telescopes still have to look through the earth's dusty and shimmery atmosphere. The best view of the sky can be seen from space itself, right outside our atmosphere. Telescopes of up to a 32-inch (0.81-meter) opening have already been flown in unmanned satellites.

But all the world's astronomers are waiting with great excitement for the space telescope to be carried into orbit in the space shuttle. This telescope with its 94-inch (2.4-meter) aperture will show details ten times as fine as any telescope has ever done on earth.

See also: ASTRONOMY, BINOCULARS, CAMERA, OBSERVATORY, RADIO TELESCOPE

Top left: A photograph taken when the world's largest optical telescope was being built. It is at Zelenchukskaya, Russia. To follow a star, it has a computer-controlled driving mechanism.

Top right: The Mount Wilson tower telescope, used for observing the sun. The telescope is built well above ground level to avoid the moving air close to the ground.

Left: An amateur reflecting telescope. It is a Newtonian type with a 9-inch (23-centimeter) main mirror. A telescope like this will show craters on the moon which are a few hundred yards across.

Astronomy

Until quite recently, people believed that the earth was the center of the universe. Now astronomers realize that our earth is only a tiny, unimportant speck in space—a speck moving around the sun. And the sun itself is only one of about 100,000 million stars in our galaxy.

From the earliest times, people have tried to find out about the strange objects—heavenly bodies—in the sky. These people watched the heavens and kept detailed records of what they saw.

Early astronomy

It was natural for them to study the heavenly bodies because these bodies were important in their everyday lives. Hunting, collecting wood for fires, and most other tasks could only be carried out in the light of the day, so the times of sunrise and sunset were important. The moon gave them a calendar they could rely on. The moon's regular change in shape, repeated every 29½ days, became known as a month. People needed a calendar so that they could plan the sowing and harvesting of their crops.

The earliest true astronomers were the ancient Babylonians in the Middle East, some 5000 years ago. But it was not until the time of the great Greek civilization that people tried to explain the things they saw in the sky. It was only then that some people began to suggest that the earth might be round and not flat. But they still agreed that the earth must be the center of the universe and that everything else in the sky circled around it.

Then came Copernicus

In 1543, a Polish scientist called Copernicus published a book in which he said that the earth and the other planets circled around the sun. He also said that the earth was spinning like a top and that the stars were immense distances away from us.

The suggestion that the earth was not the center of the universe upset many people. But in 1609, when the Italian Galileo turned his telescope to the sky and saw that the Milky Way was made up of millions of stars and that there were four moons which moved around the planet Jupiter, everyone knew that Copernicus had been right.

At about the same time, a German, Johannes Kepler, showed that the planets move in elliptical (oval) paths around the sun. Then in 1687, the great English scientist Isaac Newton explained in his law of gravitation why the planets travel around the sun as they do.

The stars

The stars (including our nearest star, the sun) are hot balls of gas that is mostly hydrogen. The enormous pressure inside them raises the temperature to millions of degrees, and in this great heat the atoms of hydrogen

1 January 10 p.m.

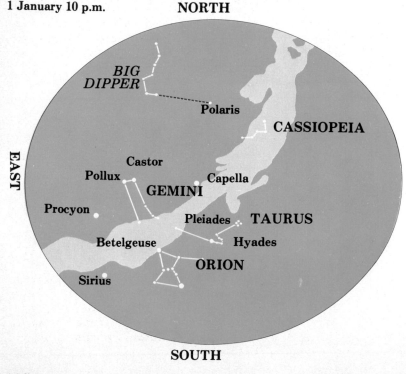

In any one place, there are stars that can be seen on clear nights. The diagram on the left shows stars that are near the northern celestial pole. This is how the sky looks in winter. Look for Orion with its belt of three stars in the south, then you can find Sirius, the brightest star in the sky. Above that is the constellation Gemini with its twin stars Castor and Pollux. The Pleiades and Hyades are star clusters. On this map you can also see the W-shaped constellation Cassiopeia. This beautiful constellation is on the edge of the Milky Way. In the far north of the map is the Big Dipper with its pointers to the Pole Star, Polaris.

110

join together in NUCLEAR REACTIONS to form helium. This releases enough energy to keep the process going as long as the hydrogen lasts.

Some stars are hotter than others. The color of a star depends on its temperature. Cool red stars may have a surface temperature below 5500 degrees F (3000 degrees C); white stars may be as hot as 90,000 degrees F (50,000 C). Our sun, at 10,000 degrees F (6000 degrees C) is yellowish.

How far away are the stars?
It is difficult to imagine how far away the stars are. They are so far away that distances have to be measured in units called LIGHT-YEARS—the distance light travels in one year (about 6,000,000,000,000 miles —9,500,000,000,000 kilometers). The nearest star, Proxima Centauri, is a little over four light-years away. The bright star Rigel in the constellation of Orion is 800 light-years away from us. Our own group of stars, called the Milky Way galaxy, is 100,000 light-years across. Other galaxies have been discovered that are thousands of millions of light-years away. This gives some idea of how enormous the whole universe is.

Star brightness
The brightness of stars as we see them is measured in what astronomers call MAGNITUDES. A star with a magnitude of 1 is very bright. It is 2½ times as bright as a magnitude 2 star. A magnitude 6 star can just be

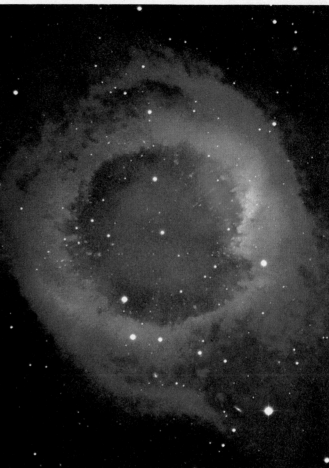

Above: The Helix Nebula is a giant red star. This beautiful nebula shows what will happen to our own sun as it expands and begins to die out.

1 July 10 p.m.

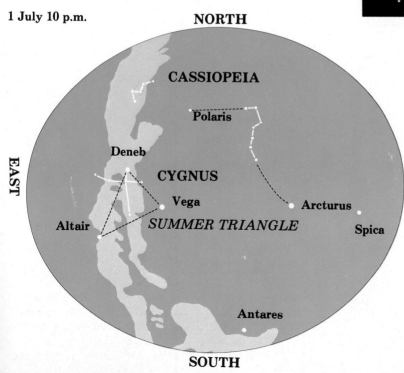

NORTH
CASSIOPEIA
Polaris
Deneb
CYGNUS
Vega
Arcturus
EAST
WEST
Altair
SUMMER TRIANGLE
Spica
Antares
SOUTH

Left: A star map of the northern sky in summer. Find the Big Dipper, part of Ursa Major. It points to the Pole Star, Polaris, near the sky's north pole. The handle of the dipper also helps you to find the bright star Arcturus. The constellation Cygnus, the Swan, makes the Summer Triangle. Its brightest star is Deneb, the others being Altair and Vega. Cygnus lies in the Milky Way. Try to find Antares in the south. This is a huge red supergiant star and is in the constellation Scorpius, the Scorpion.

seen with the naked eye. It is 100 times fainter than a 1st magnitude star. But some stars are even brighter than magnitude 1; these are given minus values. The brightest star in the sky, Sirius, is magnitude −1.47.

But the brightness of stars as we see them bears little relation to their true brightness. A nearby star looks brighter than a distant one.

The moving heavens

Because the earth is spinning on its AXIS, all the bodies we see in the sky—the sun, the planets and the stars—rise and set each day. As the earth spins from west to east, the heavenly bodies appear to travel in the opposite direction. They all rise in the east and set in the west.

However, if a photograph of the sky is taken at exactly the same time on two successive nights we can see that the stars are not in exactly the same positions. On the second night they reach their previous positions four minutes earlier. This shift in position is caused by the movement of the earth around the sun. Everything in the universe is on the move.

The constellations

At first sight, the night sky is just a jumble of stars. If we look more closely, however, we can see that many of the brightest stars form patterns that we can recognize. It is by means of these star patterns (constellations) that astronomers find their way through the heavens.

The ancient Greeks named the constellations after heroes, heroines, birds and animals—Hercules, Andromeda, Cygnus the swan, Scorpio the scorpion. A few of the constellations actually look like these images, but a great deal of imagination is needed to see the shape.

The life of a star

Stars are born from vast clouds of gas and dust. These clouds are called nebulae. Star formation starts when parts of the cloud begin to contract and form tighter blobs of gas. Each blob goes on getting smaller and denser until the temperature at its center becomes so great that NUCLEAR REACTIONS begin. The blob then begins to glow, giving out light and heat. A star has been born.

Stars spend most of their life shining in a steady way. They make energy deep inside them by turning hydrogen into helium in great nuclear reactions. This is what gives our star, the sun, its light and heat.

Toward the end of its life, a star starts to use up its hydrogen fuel more quickly. It grows bigger and brighter and grows into a red giant. Our sun will, one day in millions of years, swell up into a red giant. It will grow so big that it will swallow up Mercury, Venus and the earth. Fortunately, this is not likely to happen for about 5000 million years.

The death of a star

When a star becomes a red giant, it is nearing the end of its life. Soon the thin outer gas layers of the big star drift away, leaving nothing but a tiny, hot star called a white dwarf. White dwarf stars can be as small as our earth. The material in them is so tightly packed that a spoonful of it could weigh as much as 10 tons. After millions and millions of years the white dwarf cools down until it is no longer a shining star, just a dead lump of matter. This is how our sun will end its days.

Different kinds of stars

How long a star lives depends on how heavy it is. The heaviest stars of all—perhaps more than five times as heavy as the sun—end their days in a spectacular way. When such a star becomes a red giant, it blows apart in a nuclear explosion known as a SUPERNOVA. Its brightness increases billions of times as it throws off its outer layers far into space.

But a supernova does not always destroy itself completely. Sometimes the star's center is left behind, squeezed into a ball much smaller and denser than even a white dwarf. This is called a NEUTRON star. A spoonful

Left: What will happen when, in millions of years, the sun swells up into a huge red giant. By this time, the planets Mercury and Venus will have already been vaporized. Earth's oceans will have boiled away, but perhaps the human race, years before, will have moved to another planet.

Below: An artist's impression of a spaceship about to explore a black hole. If it gets too close it will be sucked in by the black hole's vast gravitational pull—and vanish into nothingness.

of the material in a neutron star would weigh 1000 million tons!

Neutron stars are so small that they are almost invisible to astronomers. But they give themselves away because they shoot out pulses of radio waves. Each time a neutron star spins, it sends out a flash of radio waves. These flashing neutron stars are called PULSARS. Over 300 of them have been found during the past ten years.

Black holes

If the object left behind by a supernova is more than three times heavier than the sun, it becomes quite extraordinary. The object is so dense that the inward pull of its own gravity makes it shrink more and more. After a while it shrinks so much that it vanishes and becomes what is known as a black hole. Nothing

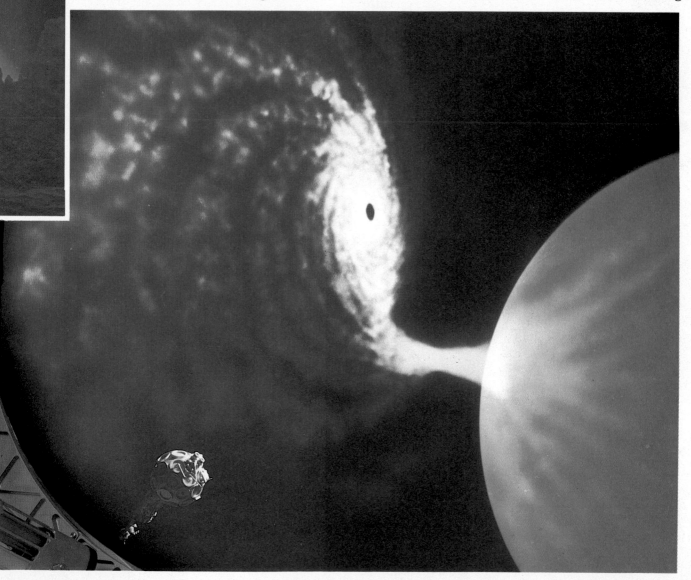

113

can escape from a black hole, not even its own light. Since no light can come out, a black hole is completely invisible.

Double stars
Most stars are not alone, like our sun. They travel in pairs or three together or more. These are called binary (double) or multiple stars.

In some double star systems, one star moves around in front of the other, blotting out its light, or ECLIPSING it. When this happens, the astronomers see a drop in the total light from the two stars. Stars like this are called eclipsing binaries. The two stars in a double system can be quite different from each other in size and brightness.

The Milky Way
Our sun is just one of about 100,000 million stars in a vast flat spiral which is our galaxy. On a clear night we can see several thousands of the stars in our galaxy with the naked eye.

In some parts of the sky there are so many stars that they appear to form a white band, which is why our galaxy is called the Milky Way. When we look up at the

Above: Stars by the million in this photograph are part of our Milky Way galaxy—stars of all sizes, ages and temperatures. The bright gas clouds are where new stars are being born.

Milky Way we are looking through the thickest part of the galaxy.

The distance right across our galaxy is about 600,000 million million miles (one million million million kilometers). It is easier to call this distance 100,000 light-years. Our sun is a tiny speck 30,000 light-years away from the center of the galaxy.

Galaxies in space
Our Milky Way galaxy is so vast that it is quite impossible for us to imagine such enormous distances. But the Milky Way is only a very ordinary galaxy among thousands of millions of galaxies stretching out through space as far as our biggest telescopes can reach.

Galaxies vary in shape. Over half are spirals, like our galaxy. A quarter are "barred spirals." These are spiral galaxies with a bar of stars across their centers. Most of the remaining galaxies are oval in shape.

The mysterious quasars

Quasars are the most powerful sources of energy we know of in the universe. They seem to be much smaller than ordinary galaxies, but they send out hundreds of times as much radiation in the form of radio waves, X-rays and ordinary light.

Quasars are unbelievably far away. The light that we see coming from them has been traveling for thousands of millions of years. So, when we look at a quasar we are looking at an object as it existed soon after the universe was born. Astronomers can find no quasars in our part of the universe. Perhaps they are objects that were formed and died away when our universe was new.

The Big Bang

In 1929, the American astronomer Edwin Hubble made an astounding discovery. He found that all the galaxies were moving away from us and from each other at high speed. This meant that the whole universe must be expanding like a balloon being blown up. If we paint spots on a balloon to represent the galaxies and then blow it up, the spots will grow farther and farther apart.

How the universe began

Edwin Hubble's discovery pointed the way to our present-day ideas on how the universe began. Most scientists now believe that the universe started with an enormous explosion called the Big Bang that sent material flying in all directions. Before the Big Bang, all the matter in the universe was squeezed into one small spot.

Astronomers have worked out from the speed of expansion of the universe that the Big Bang took place about 20,000 million years ago. But this is only a theory. We still have no idea what was there before the explosion or what caused it. Perhaps we never will.

Below: Different objects in the sky send out different radiations. Only light waves and short radio waves can get through the earth's atmosphere to ground level. Astronomers using infrared film work in high mountains or from aircraft. For other wavelengths we need an observatory in orbit, above the atmosphere.

See also: ASTRONOMICAL TELESCOPE, DOPPLER EFFECT, JUPITER, MARS, MERCURY, MOON, NEPTUNE AND PLUTO, OBSERVATORY, PLANETARIUM, RADIO TELESCOPE, SATURN, SOLAR SYSTEM, SUN, URANUS, VENUS

long wavelength radio   radio   infrared   visible light   ultraviolet   X-ray   gamma ray

Ionosphere

Ozone layer

Carbon dioxide and water vapor

Atoms and Molecules

Everything around us is made up of particles called atoms. These are so tiny that a line of 50 million hydrogen atoms would be only about 0.4 inches (1 centimeter) long. Atoms are formed from combinations of even smaller particles called protons, electrons and neutrons. Atoms combine to form particles called molecules.

Elements and atomic numbers

All the physical and chemical properties of a substance depend on its atoms and the way they are arranged within that substance. Any substance made up from atoms all containing the same number of PROTONS is called an ELEMENT.

The number of protons in each atom is known as the atomic number of the element. Atomic numbers range from 1 (hydrogen) to more than 100. Carbon, for example, has an atomic number of 6, oxygen has an atomic number of 8, and lead, 82.

Electricity and the atom

The particles that make up atoms have different electrical properties. Protons each have a positive electrical charge. Electrons, however, have an equal but opposite (negative) charge. Neutrons have no charge at all. As a normal atom has equal numbers of protons and electrons, their charges cancel each other out exactly. So no overall charge can be noticed.

In order to give a substance an electrical charge, we must upset the balance of protons and electrons in some way. A simple way to do this is by means of FRICTION.

For example, if you rub a balloon with a piece of silk, electrons will be transferred from the silk to the balloon. The balloon, now having an excess of electrons, will be negatively charged. And the silk, having more protons than electrons, will be positively charged.

One property of charged objects is that they attract uncharged objects. You can show that the balloon and silk are charged by holding them near feathers, small pieces of paper, or other light objects. These will jump

Below: A substance is a solid, liquid or gas depending on the energy of its atoms or molecules. Solids have slow-moving particles that pack tightly together.

Right: A hydrogen atom has a nucleus of one proton, with one electron orbiting it.

Far right: A neon atom, with ten electrons, ten protons and ten neutrons.

Below: Atoms of helium (left) and lithium-7 (right).

Below far right: A water molecule consisting of two hydrogen and one oxygen atoms linked by orbiting electrons.

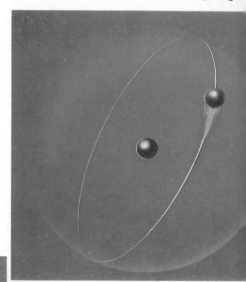

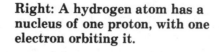

gas

molecules

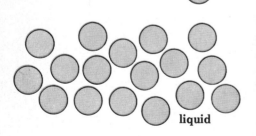

liquid

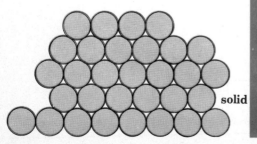

solid

up and cling to the body until it loses its charge.

Isotopes and mass number

Although the atoms of a given element all contain the same number of protons, different numbers of neutrons are usually present. In natural carbon, for example, most of the atoms contain six neutrons. But about one percent of the atoms each contain seven neutrons. These different types of atom of the same element are called ISOTOPES. The isotopes of an element all have the same chemical properties, although some of their physical properties (such as melting and boiling points) differ.

The MASS NUMBER of an atom is the total number of protons and neutrons that it contains. (Electrons are so light and add so little to the mass of an atom that they are ignored.) Scientists use this number when referring to a particular isotope. For example, the common natural isotope of carbon, which contains six protons and six neutrons, is called carbon-12. The rarer natural isotope, which contains an extra neutron, is called carbon-13.

Right: Atoms of different elements can combine to form a wide range of more complex substances called compounds. Each of the compounds shown here is made up from two or more of the elements shown on the far right-hand side of the diagram.

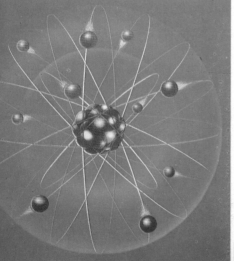

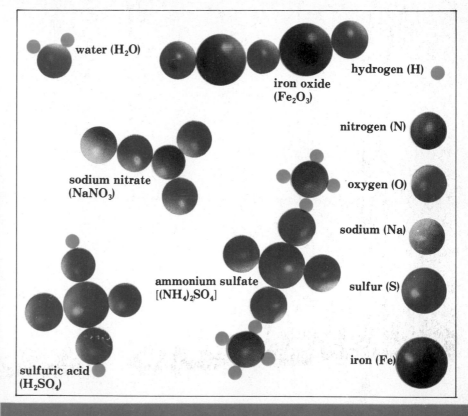

water (H_2O)

iron oxide (Fe_2O_3)

hydrogen (H)

nitrogen (N)

sodium nitrate ($NaNO_3$)

oxygen (O)

sodium (Na)

ammonium sulfate [$(NH_4)_2SO_4$]

sulfur (S)

sulfuric acid (H_2SO_4)

iron (Fe)

Besides the natural isotopes, various artificial isotopes can be produced by NUCLEAR REACTIONS. These are reactions involving changes in the nucleus, or center, of an atom. The isotopes carbon-10, carbon-11, carbon-14 and carbon-15 can be produced in this way.

Atomic weight

Whereas the mass number of an atom is always a whole number, the atomic weight of an element is not. The atomic weight is the average mass number of a known mixture of isotopes. Normally, this is the mixture that occurs naturally. Natural carbon, for example, contains mostly carbon-12 atoms, with a small proportion of carbon-13. As a result, its atomic weight is 12.011.

Molecules and molecular weight

Atoms usually occur in groups called molecules. A molecule of hydrogen gas, for example, consists of two hydrogen atoms joined together. Scientists represent such a molecule by the chemical formula H_2. Similarly, a molecule of oxygen gas has the chemical formula O_2. This shows that the molecule contains two atoms of oxygen.

The molecular weight of a substance is the sum of the atomic weights of all the atoms in one molecule. So, as hydrogen and oxygen molecules each contain two atoms, their molecular weights are double their atomic weights.

Compounds

The elements, such as carbon, hydrogen and oxygen, are simple substances. Compounds are more complex (difficult) substances. Their molecules contain atoms of more than one element. Water, for example, is a compound which is made of the elements hydrogen and oxygen. One molecule of water contains two atoms of hydrogen and one atom of oxygen. So scientists represent this molecule by the chemical formula H_2O.

Most molecules of compounds are more complex. A sulfuric acid molecule, for example, has two hydrogen atoms, one sulfur atom and four oxygen atoms. The formula for a molecule of this acid is H_2SO_4. But this is still a fairly simple compound compared with the giant protein molecules in our bodies. Most protein molecules contain hundreds or thousands of atoms and have molecular weights ranging up to about ten million. However, they are still too small to be seen with the naked eye.

Solids, liquids and gases

Molecules are always moving. In solids, the molecules are packed together tightly, and they vibrate about fixed points. Strong forces of attraction between the molecules prevent them from moving past each other. This is why a solid object tends to keep its shape.

Most solids can be changed into liquid form by heating. Heat makes the molecules move faster. Eventually, they are able to move past each other to new positions. As a result, the substance can change shape and flow readily. In this liquid form, some molecules have enough energy to break through the surface and escape. This is called EVAPORATION.

Further heating causes the molecules to move even faster. When the boiling point of the liquid is reached, the molecules gain enough energy to move about almost freely. The liquid then changes into a gas.

Another thing that can cause a substance to change from one physical state to another is its pressure. For example, some gases turn into liquids when their molecules are forced together by an increase in pressure.

Above: Scientists use devices called bubble chambers to watch fast-moving subatomic particles. The spirals in this bubble chamber photograph show the paths of electrons, knocked out of atoms by high-speed particles.

Left: In this bubble chamber, particles form trails of bubbles in liquid hydrogen at −254 degrees C (−425 degrees F).

This happens in a typical camping stove. Gas, such as butane, in a liquid form is stored in a cylinder under pressure. When a valve is opened, the pressure is reduced and the butane comes out as a gas.

Inside the atom

By the 1890s, a great deal was known about the behavior of atoms. But not much was known about their structure for they were too small to see, even under the most powerful microscope. However, certain electrical experiments had provided an important clue. A high VOLTAGE was found to produce invisible rays streaming between two metal plates in an empty, sealed tube.

The physicist J. J. Thomson showed that the rays consisted of negatively charged particles. These became known as electrons. It was correctly assumed that the electrons came from the atoms of the metal plate emitting the rays. But just exactly how the electrons were arranged within an atom still remained a mystery.

Rutherford's reasons

In 1911, Ernest Rutherford, who had studied with Thomson, put forward his theory of the structure of the atom. Earlier experiments had shown that positively charged particles are scattered when fired at a thin film of atoms (as in very fine gold foil). Rutherford reasoned that a positive nucleus within the gold atoms turns away the particles. He concluded that the atom has a positive nucleus surrounded by a cloud of electrons.

Rutherford's model of the atom has formed the basis of our understanding ever since. We can think of the atom as a miniature solar system. Electrons orbit the nucleus, just like planets moving around the sun. This explanation is perfectly satisfactory for many purposes. But some experiments reveal that the atom is really more complicated. Niels Bohr showed that electrons orbit only at certain distances from the nucleus. So the atom can be thought of as having a series of invisible "shells" around it. Electrons orbit only on the shells, but sometimes jump from one shell to another.

How many particles?

In 1932, James Chadwick discovered a particle that had no electrical charge, the neutron. For a short while, this seemed to complete the story of the atom. But, in 1934, it was suspected that other particles produce the forces that hold protons and neutrons together in the nucleus. These binding particles are now called MESONS. This discovery prompted the search for new particles, and in fact 30 were found over the next 20 years.

Since then, the machines called accelerators, with which scientists probe the atom, have become extremely powerful. The result has been the discovery of hundreds of other kinds of particles. So there are now even more questions to answer about the atom than ever before.

See also: A-BOMB, ACCELERATORS, BUBBLE CHAMBER, CARBON, MICROSCOPE, PROTEINS

Automobiles

The automobile is one of the most important inventions of all time. It has become the world's basic transport machine and allows us to travel almost anywhere in comfort. In the United States twice as many cars are built as babies are born in one year.

There are many differences in automobile design, but here we will describe a "standard" model. It has an engine at the front which drives the back wheels, and simple suspension, brake and steering systems.

The heart of the car is the engine. Nowadays, this is a highly efficient machine that converts liquid gasoline into energy which turns the wheels.

Gasoline is drawn from the tank by a fuel pump, driven by the engine. The gasoline goes to the carburetor where it is turned into a VAPOR—a mixture of gasoline and air. The amount of gasoline that is mixed with air depends on how far the accelerator pedal is pressed down.

The engine

The gas-air mixture is fed to each of the engine's cylinders in turn, through the inlet valves. The mixture is compressed (squeezed) by the rising piston in the cylinder. An electrical spark from a spark plug at the top of the cylinder then makes the mixture explode.

This explosion forces the piston down the cylinder, and on its return up the cylinder again, the piston pushes out the burned gases. They go out through an exhaust valve, which opens at just the right moment, and pass through the muffler and the exhaust pipe.

Each of the automobile's pistons drives a connecting rod. The connecting rods are joined to the crankshaft and turn the up-and-down movements of the pistons into the circular movement of the crankshaft. At the end of the crankshaft is a heavy flywheel which keeps the engine running smoothly.

Right: The Model T Ford was the world's first mass-produced automobile. Fifteen million of them were built between 1908 and 1927.

Getting the power to the wheels

An automobile is heavy. Standing still or at slow speed, it takes a lot to move it. The transmission passes the power from the engine to the drive shaft that turns the wheels. The transmission can reduce the speed to increase the turning power, or reduce the turning power to increase the speed. To set a car in motion or to push it up a hill, the transmission gives less speed and more turning power to the drive shaft. When the automobile is cruising along a level highway, the transmission gives more speed and less turning power to the drive shaft.

With a manual transmission, the driver moves the transmission gears by using a lever called a gear shift. He or she puts the lever in first gear to start off, then into second, third and fourth gear as the automobile

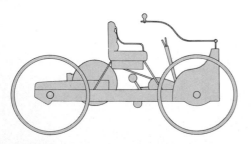

Before 1900, the parts of an automobile were arranged wherever they would fit.

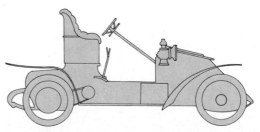

By 1910, most cars had an engine at the front, seats in the middle and rear-wheel drive.

gains speed. (Many cars now have a fifth gear.) The driver can also use a reverse gear for going backward. The driver has to operate the clutch for each gear change to disconnect the engine from the transmission.

With automatic transmission, the speed of the drive shaft is chosen automatically. The driver does not have to use a clutch pedal, and there is no gear shift.

The drive shaft is a steel tube that takes the power from the transmission back to the differential via universal joints. Universal joints are made so that the rear axles can bump up and down without breaking the drive shaft. The differential is a set of gears that allows the two separate shafts turning the back wheels to turn at different speeds. This is necessary because, as the automobile goes around a corner, the outside wheel goes faster than the one on the inside of the corner.

The suspension

To make the automobile comfortable to ride in, the wheels are attached to the body by a suspension system. There are several types of suspension, but in most cars, springs and shock absorbers are used.

Leaf springs are made up of layers of flexible material shaped like a bow. Each end of the bow is connected to the car's chassis, while the center is joined to the axle. Coil springs are strong springs which are connected directly between the axle and the chassis. To avoid "bouncing," shock absorbers are put into the springing system to cut down the movement of the springs.

The brakes

On each of the four wheels is a brake drum or disk. When the driver presses down the brake pedal, a pair of brake shoes expands and rubs against the inside of the drum; or, in the case of the disk brake, pads squeeze the disk between them. Both shoes and pads are made of high friction material which causes the wheels to slow.

Both kinds of brakes work by HYDRAULIC pressure. When the brake pedal is pressed, liquid is forced out of a master cylinder into brake cylinders at each wheel. These cylinders work the shoes and pads.

The steering

The automobile is steered by the front wheels. The steering wheel turns a shaft which is connected at its bottom end to steering gears. These gears move rods which are pulled to the left or right and move the wheels. Some cars have hydraulic power steering to make turning the steering wheel easier.

The ignition system

The spark at the spark plug must be very accurately timed. This is done by the ignition system. The electric current for the spark comes from the battery. The current is passed to the distributor which gives a short burst of current at the exact moment needed for ignition at each cylinder.

Of course, a machine that works by a series of explosions becomes very hot. Most engines are cooled by water which is pumped around the cylinder block by a water pump, and through a radiator which gets rid of the unwanted heat. Behind the radiator is a fan which

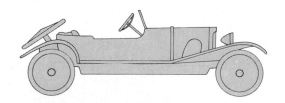

By 1920, automobiles had doors and windshields. They were larger and lower.

During the 1930s the passengers were closed in and the body line became more "swoopy."

draws air through the radiator. Both the fan and the water pump are driven by a belt from the crankshaft.

The story of the automobile

The first real automobile, driven by a gasoline engine, appeared in the 1880s. But people had been trying to make steam-driven cars for a hundred years before that. It is usually said that the first man to sit behind the controls of a self-propelled car was the French engineer Nicolas Cugnot. In 1770 he built a three-

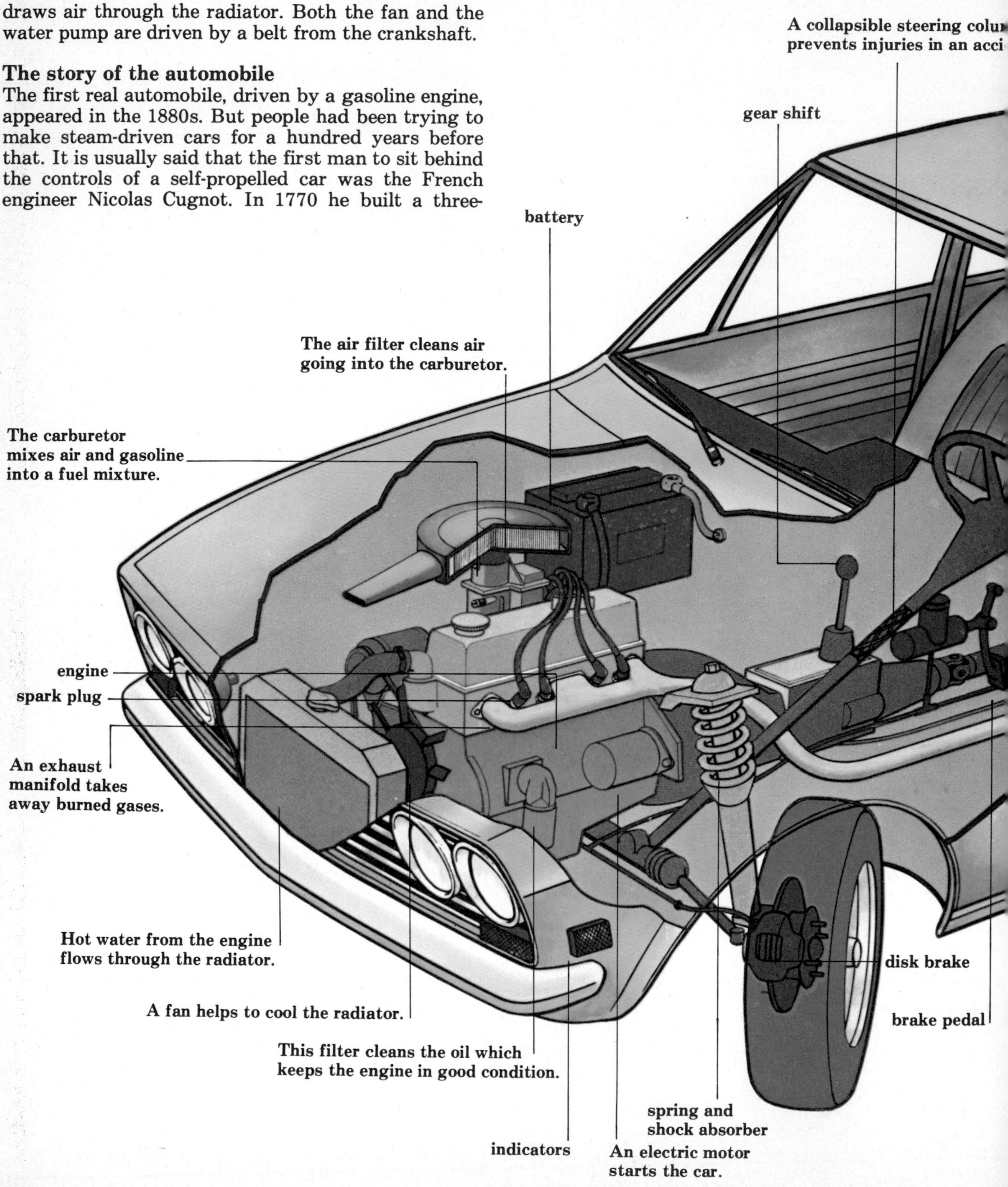

A collapsible steering colum prevents injuries in an acci

gear shift

battery

The air filter cleans air going into the carburetor.

The carburetor mixes air and gasoline into a fuel mixture.

engine

spark plug

An exhaust manifold takes away burned gases.

Hot water from the engine flows through the radiator.

A fan helps to cool the radiator.

This filter cleans the oil which keeps the engine in good condition.

disk brake

brake pedal

indicators

spring and shock absorber

An electric motor starts the car.

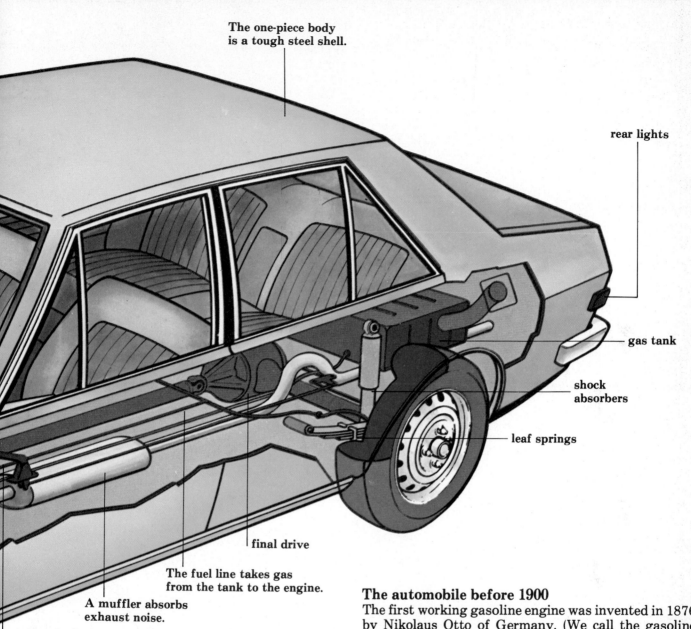

The one-piece body is a tough steel shell.

rear lights

gas tank

shock absorbers

leaf springs

final drive

The fuel line takes gas from the tank to the engine.

A muffler absorbs exhaust noise.

parking brake

wheeled machine driven by steam which reached a speed of 6 mph (10 km/h).

But steam was not the answer for powering the automobile. Steam engines had to carry around a boiler and a big water tank as well as the engine and fuel for the fire.

People also tried electric cars in the 1890s, but they didn't work very well either. The batteries were too heavy and they didn't last long enough with one charge.

The automobile before 1900

The first working gasoline engine was invented in 1876 by Nikolaus Otto of Germany. (We call the gasoline engine an internal combustion engine.) Then, following Otto's work, Karl Benz and Gottlieb Daimler, working quite separately, built the world's first cars fitted with internal combustion engines. The Benz of 1885 was a three-wheeled car and had an open, wooden two-seater body. It had one wheel at the front and this wheel was steered by a tiller. The two large rear wheels were driven by chains. These chains were turned by a single-cylinder gasoline engine. The engine produced about ½ horsepower and drove the car at about 8 to 10 mph (13 to 16 km/h).

Gottlieb and Daimler's car was a converted carriage, with four wheels. It had a single-cylinder engine which produced 1½ horsepower.

By 1900, various automobile designs had appeared. Inventions included the carburetor, the steering wheel, the pneumatic tire, engines with more than one cylinder, the gate gearchange and the radiator.

The first motor race was held in 1895 over a distance of 750 miles (1200 kilometers) from Paris to Bordeaux in France. It was won by a 4-horsepower, twin-cylinder car made by Panhard and Lavassor. The race took 48 hours and the winner averaged 15 mph (24 km/h), even though he fell asleep at the wheel on the return to Paris.

Many Americans experimented with gasoline-powered vehicles. Among them were Charles and Frank Duryea, who built the first successful American gasoline-powered automobile.

The automobile between 1900 and 1920

Better engines gave higher road speeds. This made designers produce better brakes and transmission systems. The early brakes were the same as those used on carriages and on bicycles. A solid block of wood, leather or metal was pushed against the wheel rims by a hand lever. Then came brake drums in which a band of material closed on drums attached to the rear wheels.

There were two other important changes in the early 1900s. Gasoline prices dropped sharply after the discovery of rich oilfields in Texas. And mass-production started off the great American automobile industry.

In 1908, the first Model T from Henry Ford came off the production line. By 1911, Ford of America was producing 1000 automobiles a day. During the next 19 years, over 15 million Model T Fords were made.

General Motors started up in 1908 when several American motor manufacturers were joined together—makers such as Buick, Cadillac, Oldsmobile and Oakland. General Motors became the world's largest automobile manufacturer.

1920 to today

Between the two World Wars, mass production of automobiles became well-established. There was a wide range of cheap, reliable and comfortable vehicles. Engines became more powerful and quieter, and other improvements included four-wheel brakes, windshield

The distributor sends "sparking power" to the spark plugs.

Beneath this air filter is the carburetor which mixes air and gas into a mixture that will burn.

The fuel burns in these cylinders and the force pushes the pistons down. Cylinders fire at different times.

The crankshaft sends turning power to the wheels by way of the gearbox, propeller shaft, final drive and axles.

Pistons slide up and down to turn the crankshaft.

The big end of the connecting rod, which joins the piston to the crankshaft, swings around like a foot on a bicycle pedal.

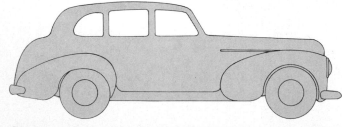

Shortly before and after World War II, cars became heavier and more rounded.

Automobiles of the 1950s were made simpler. They had a "three box" shape.

How one automaker has developed its line. The 1953 Buick Skylark on the left had a 2-speed automatic transmission. It did 12.8 miles (20.6 kilometers) to the gallon and weighed 4315 pounds (1957 kilograms).

The 1971 Buick Electra below had a 3-speed automatic transmission. It did 11.36 miles (18.3 kilometers) per gallon and weighed 4740 pounds (2150 kilograms).

The 1982 Buick Century on the right had a 3-speed automatic transmission. It did 22.48 miles (36.1 kilometers) per gallon and weighed 2723 pounds (1235 kilograms).

wipers, shatterproof glass, independent suspension and balloon tires. In 1937, General Motors produced a medium-priced automatic transmission.

American manufacturers began to make powerful luxury automobiles. In Europe, makers turned to small low-priced cars such as the Austin 7 in England, the Fiat 500 in Italy and the Volkswagen in Germany.

After World War II, automobiles became longer, lower and more elaborate. Curved glass was used in windshields and a great deal of chromium plating was used. The tubeless tire came in 1948. In the early 1950s came power steering, disc brakes and, of course, all the time man was influenced by the desire to go faster.

Automobiles in the future
It is likely that the gasoline-driven car will certainly still be produced over the next few years. Experiments, however, are underway to find a cheaper fuel that will cause less pollution. Cars powered by electricity are being developed and may well be the cars of the future.

See also: BRAKE, CARBURETOR, CLUTCH, DIESEL ENGINE, ELECTRIC VEHICLES, EXHAUST SYSTEMS, IGNITION SYSTEMS, INTERNAL COMBUSTION ENGINE, POWER STEERING, SPARK PLUG, SPEEDOMETER, SUPERCHARGER, TIRE, WANKEL ENGINE

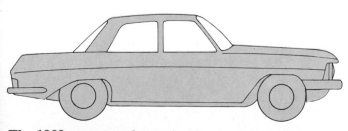

The 1960s saw cars becoming larger, lower and heavier. They had simpler, straighter lines.

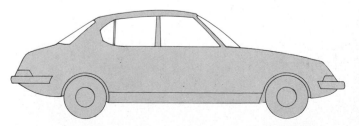

During the late 1970s, automobiles became more compact. Manufacturers concentrated on economy.

Aviation History

Ever since people first watched birds swooping through the sky, they have longed to fly. For hundreds of years, people tried to fit wings to their own bodies or tried to make flying machines with flapping wings. By the 17th century it was recognized that people would never fly like the birds.

The main trouble with the early airplane designs was that none of the inventors seemed to have any idea about how they should be controlled once they left the ground. All the would-be aviators thought that, if only they could build the right kind of machine, they could just get in and fly off. One or two of these early pioneers almost succeeded.

Powered by steam

In 1890, Clément Ader, a Frenchman, took off in a steam-powered plane that he had built. But he could not keep it in the air. In 1894, Sir Hiram Maxim, an American who had become a British citizen, built a huge steam-powered machine. It had two wings (a biplane) and two engines. The heavy machine only managed to lift off the ground for a few seconds.

Below: Wilbur Wright's flight in Europe in 1908.

Getting off the ground

Between 1891 and 1896, the German, Otto Lilienthal, made more than 2000 successful flights in gliders. He took off by running down small hills, just like the modern hang-glider pilots. Once in the air, Lilienthal could control his gliders by shifting his weight from side to side and from front to rear. In 1896 Lilienthal lost control when his glider was upset by a sudden gust of wind, and he swooped to his death.

A pupil of Lilienthal's, Samuel P. Langley, Secretary of the Smithsonian Institution in Washington, had demonstrated a large working model airplane and was given money by the U.S. Army to build a full-size machine. He decided to launch it by catapult from a houseboat on the Potomac River, but it crashed on take-off. Langley repaired his gasoline-powered plane, but it crashed again. This caused the newspapers to laugh at the whole idea of flying machines. But we know now that Langley was very close to success.

The first real flight

Two brothers, Orville and Wilbur Wright from Dayton, Ohio, had been interested in flying from boyhood. They

built up a bicycle-making business in their home town and used the money they made to experiment with gliders. The brothers built three gliders and flew them successfully on the sand hills at Kitty Hawk in North Carolina.

In 1903 they went to Kitty Hawk with a biplane powered by a 4-cylinder gasoline engine which they had built themselves. For a time, the brothers had been searching for an engine to put into their latest glider. They needed an engine that was powerful enough but light. Automobile engines of the time were not right, so they built their own engine. It produced 12 horsepower but was still quite heavy at 15 pounds (7 kilograms) to the horsepower. It had its cylinders set in-line like those of a small automobile engine.

The wings of the plane were flimsy wooden frames covered with cloth. The engine turned two wooden propellers behind the wings. The pilot lay on his stomach with wire string attached to his waist. The wires went to each wing tip, and by moving his hips the pilot could twist the wing tips and balance the plane in flight.

On December 17, 1903, Orville Wright took off in this plane, which the brothers had called the *Flyer*. The flight lasted some 12 seconds and covered a distance of 120 feet (37 meters). Later that same day, on a fourth flight, Wilbur stayed in the air for 59 seconds and covered a distance of 852 feet (260 meters), against a strong wind. Man had at last conquered the air.

Aviation takes off

From that day on aviation never looked back. In 1909, Louis Blériot flew from France to England in one of his monoplanes (single-winged aircraft), and a month later the first great flying meeting was held in Reims, France. One of the top speed prizes at this event was awarded to the American, Glenn Curtiss, who traveled at 47 mph (77 km/h).

By September 1913, this record had been raised to 126.6 mph (204 km/h). The Deperdussin Company in France had built the first successful airplane of monocoque construction—the body of the plane (fuselage) had a tube-like shape. This shape of fuselage did not need so many braces to hold it together, so it was lighter.

Below: Two posters, one showing an early, unsuccessful, aircraft design and the other the first air fair in France.

World War I

By the beginning of World War I, when powered flight was just ten years old, the use of airplanes in war was still vague. While there were many who could see the advantages of putting an observer above the enemy line, others saw no military use for the flying machine and some even complained that the noise would upset the cavalry! However, both sides began to use them for general overseas reconnaissance duties once war broke out.

These early warplanes were called "scouts." Very soon enemy scouts began to confront one another in the air, shooting wildly with rifles and pistols. Machine guns were soon fitted to protect the scouts, and these were eventually able to fire through the propeller arc without damaging the blades. The pilots could use their planes like guns, twisting and turning to aim at the enemy, or to avoid his fire.

New aircraft were developed to cope with the stress of combat flying, and the flimsy underpowered box-kites gave way to sturdy, lightweight biplanes built for fighting, such as the British Sopwith Camel and German Fokker D VII. In 1918 came the first all-metal fighter, the Junkers CLI.

Above: Charles Lindbergh with his plane, *Spirit of St. Louis,* **in which he flew nonstop from New York to Paris.**

The bombing airplane

Gradually, different types of aircraft were developed for different roles. In the early days, scouts over enemy positions had started dropping iron spikes and grenades, a method first used by Italian airmen against the Turks in Africa in 1911. Before long, larger bombs were produced—with bigger planes needed to carry them.

By the end of fighting in 1918, German Gotha bombers had dropped bombs several times on Britain, and the British had developed the Handley Page V/1500, a huge four-engined bomber capable of carrying 1000 pounds (453 kilograms) of bombs to Berlin, or up to 3½ tons of explosive at shorter ranges.

In just four years, the airplane had advanced from a flimsy flying platform to an efficient fighting machine.

Progress in the 1920s

After the war, airplane designers began to use a new form of construction called stressed-skin. Although the

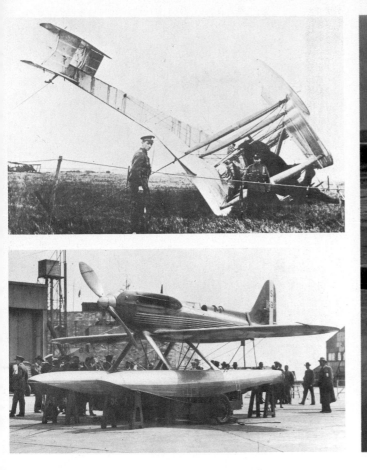

planes had a skeleton of spars, ribs and frame, the skin of the fuselage and wings was metal. This meant that the airframe (the basic plane without engines) could be very strong, light and streamlined. It allowed designers to make monoplane wings that were quite thin and did not need any bracing wires.

Famous flights

The years after the war saw many famous flights. In 1919, John Alcock and Arthur Whitten-Brown flew a converted Vickers-Vimy bomber from Newfoundland to Ireland in 16 hours 12 minutes—the first transatlantic flight. In 1926, Richard E. Byrd and Floyd Bennett flew a Fokker 3-engined plane nonstop from Spitzbergen in Norway to the North Pole and back, a distance of 1545 miles (2486 kilometers). Then, in May 1927, came the most famous flight of them all. Charles A. Lindbergh flew a Ryan monoplane, *Spirit of St. Louis*, from New York City to Paris, a distance of 3600 miles (5800 kilometers) in 33½ hours.

The 1930s

The 1930s brought many new ideas in aircraft design. Hinged flaps were added to the rear of the wings to

Left above: A not so happy landing for Alcock and Brown's Vickers Vimy after its historic flight in 1919.

Left below: The Supermarine S.6B seaplane which was an important influence on the design of the later Spitfire.

Above: The Douglas Dakota played an important part as a war plane and a passenger plane.

increase lift and resistance at low speeds and allow the new planes to land more slowly and use shorter airfields. Landing gear was made to retract (fold back) inside the plane, and so reduce resistance and increase speed. Engines were streamlined with casings called cowlings. New radio devices helped pilots to find their way at night or in bad weather.

By the end of the 1930s, wood, fabric and wire construction had almost disappeared. Most of the new planes were twin-engine types, but four-engine machines were beginning to appear. Aircraft such as the Boeing 247 and the Douglas DC series changed the face of air transportation. These machines were quite large and carried enough navigational and landing aids to make them safe in most weather conditions.

Above: Three different types of airliner: the Boeing 707 (foreground), a long-range airliner which entered service in 1958; the Caravelle (middle) a medium-range airliner introduced in 1959; and the "Jumbo"—the Boeing 747, a massive airliner which came into regular use in 1970.

World War II

Like World War I, World War II saw rapid advances in the progress of aviation. Because of the terrifying effects of bombing on civilian populations during World War I, many people believed that war could be won simply by bombing enemy cities. Designers, therefore, concentrated on medium- and long-range aircraft carrying a lot of bombs.

However, most aircraft ended up as a compromise between the need to defend themselves by being small, light and fast, yet being large enough to carry an effective load. These planes were not really suitable for fighting, and as war loomed both sides began to equip themselves with high-speed, well-armed fighters for defense, such as the Spitfire 1 and Messerschmitt Bf109.

In 1940 came the first four-engine heavy bomber, the Short Stirling, which was soon followed by other types, notably the legendary Avro Lancaster and Boeing B17 Fortress which were used in large groups in the day and night raids over Germany.

Aircraft carriers played a major part in World War II, especially in the Pacific when Japan and the United States entered the war. These mobile airfields took the air battle close to the enemy, and in 1942 the U.S. launched a bombing raid against cities in Japan from the carrier *U.S.S. Hornet.*

Jetting ahead

However, World War II also saw the introduction of something unheard of at that time—planes without propellers! In 1939, the Germans flew their jet-powered Heinkel 178 for the first time. Jet engine research was going on in other countries, and in May 1942 the British followed with the Gloster Whittle, named after the engine designer, and in the same year the U.S. produced the twin-jet Bell XP 29A.

By 1944, combat jets were beginning to appear over Europe, notably the German Me 262 and the British Meteor. The Meteor was never used in air-to-air combat, for fear the Germans might capture one.

Modern war planes

The jet warplane continued to develop after World War II, and during the Korean war in 1950 the first jet versus jet fighter battles took place. In 1947 Captain Chuck Yaeger had flown supersonic—that is past the speed of sound—in the rocket-motor Bell X-1, and by the late 1950s several of the world's leading airforces were equipped with planes able to go supersonic in level flight.

With the development of rockets, the long-range bomber was largely replaced by missiles that could take devastating atomic weapons to the other side of the earth. Meanwhile, electronic air navigation and weapon guidance systems are becoming increasingly complex, using computers to guide planes and missiles to their targets. As individual aircraft become more expensive to produce, so has the variety of tasks they have to perform become greater.

A new generation of Multi Role Combat Aircraft (MRCAs) have begun to emerge, capable of air-to-air combat and defense, medium-range bombing, ground attack and reconnaissance. With the introduction of vertical takeoff aircraft, the combat plane of today is even more flexible, capable of operating from limited spaces such as farmyards, highways and carriers at sea.

The age of the airliner
Air transportation still relied on propeller-driven aircraft until the appearance of the de Havilland Comet airliner in 1949. By 1957, the Boeing 707, the Douglas DC8 and the Soviet Tu-104 were in full production. By the 1960s the jet had swept propellers off most of the main long-haul passenger routes.

Below: The first supersonic airliner, Concorde, which can fly at speeds of up to 1335 mph (2150 km/h) and up to 60,000 feet (18,300 meters). It has made the world seem a lot smaller as it can travel from New York to London in just three hours—half the time of a normal plane!

Faster and faster
In 1970 PanAm put into service the first of a new generation of giant transports called wide-body airplanes. The cabins were 20 feet (6 meters) wide and seated 10 passengers across. The Boeing 747 could take up to 500 passengers and fly them in comfort anywhere in the world. Most of these big jets fly at a height of around 30,000 feet (2743 meters) at a cruising speed of over 500 mph (800 km/h).

Supersonic transport
To improve on normal passenger jet speeds, a new kind of plane, the supersonic transport (SST) was designed. The Anglo-French *Concorde* can fly at twice the speed of sound, faster than the speed of a rifle bullet. It has a delta (triangular) shape which is also used in some types of fighter aircraft.

Supersonic passenger aircraft are, however, very expensive to run. It remains to be seen whether this kind of plane will point the way to aircraft design in the future, or whether the larger, slower planes will finally win the day.

See also: AIRPLANES, HANG GLIDING, JET ENGINE, SUPERSONIC FLIGHT, VTOL

Avionics

Avionics is a word that comes from AVIation and electrONICS—the technology of electronics used in airplanes. The cockpit of a modern airliner is a mass of electronics—all designed to make flying safer and more comfortable.

The automatic pilot

The automatic pilot is an instrument that can tell if there is any change in the way an airplane is flying—direction, pitch (whether the nose of the airplane is pointing slightly up or down) and roll (one wingtip lower than the other). If there is a change, the autopilot moves the controls of the airplane to make the proper correction.

It works with a system of two gyroscopes, one to correct the direction, and the other the pitch and roll of the plane.

An autopilot is much better than a human at keeping the plane flying level and straight. It can also be linked to a radio navigation system on the ground to lock the airplane on to an instrument landing system (ILS).

Inertial navigation

Intercontinental airplanes often use Inertial Navigation Systems (INS). The way they work is to add up every change in direction and speed. If this is done

Immediately after takeoff, the pilot follows a "Standard Instrument Departure" (SID)—a map of air routes between radio beacons. In this case, the aircraft is told to fly to the 159 radial (line) coming from the VOR radio beacon. It must fly on this line, climbing to cross the beacon at, say, 3000 feet (900 meters).

VOR radio waves

159° radial

VOR beacon

dial reading 280°

needle reading 339°

airport

Remember: there are 360 degrees in a circle, so half a circle has 180 degrees. The 159° radial seen from the plane becomes 339° (159°+180°).

The VOR dial in the instrument panel looks like a compass. But instead of pointing north, its needle shows the direction of the VOR beacon it is tuned to. The dial itself shows the direction the plane is heading. VOR stands for VHF Omnidirectional Range—it broadcasts VHF radio signals in all directions.

The flight crew can find the beacon by following any of the 360 VOR signals it sends out. The pilot can join the VOR direction information to the autopilot and the plane will automatically fly to the VOR beacon. VOR beacons are placed at intervals along the most used air corridors and are a very important part of the air navigation system.

starting from a known position, then the airplane's position can be worked out at any time. The INS uses gyroscopes and accelerometers (devices that sense changes of speed) to detect and measure the changes. The sums needed to work out the airplane's position are done by a microcomputer.

A tiny mistake throughout a long flight can add up to an INS being way out by the end. This is known as "drift." It is often overcome by having more than one INS on board and making checks to see if the results agree.

Direction finding

Most aircraft carry VHF (Very High Frequency) Omnidirectional Range (VOR) equipment for direction finding. The VOR ground beacon sends out radio signals in all directions. These are broken up into 360 separate beams, one for each degree of the compass. The pilot can pick up one of these VOR signals.

Above: A combined VOR and DME beacon. The outer ring is the VOR. The center pole is the DME.

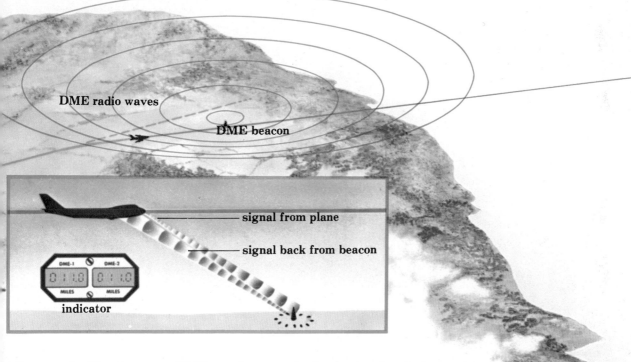

DME radio waves

DME beacon

signal from plane

signal back from beacon

DME-1   DME-2

0 1 1.0   0 1 1.0

MILES   MILES

indicator

The captain flies from one VOR beacon to the next, as shown in his SID instructions. He can also use DME (Distance Measuring Equipment) beacons. A transmitter on the plane sends a radio signal to the DME beacon it is tuned to. When the beacon picks up the signal, it sends back a signal of its own within millionths of a second. The further the plane is from the beacon, the longer it takes before the receiver picks up the reply from the beacon. An indicator in the plane shows how far it is to the DME beacon. VOR and DME beacons act like signposts, showing the roads in the sky. On shorter journeys, planes follow VOR and DME beacons. For longer journeys they also use the Inertial Navigation System (INS).

On picking up a signal, the plane's instruments show the direction of the beacon. By giving the direction information to the autopilot, the plane is guided in the direction of the beacon. There are VOR beacons conveniently placed on the most used air routes.

Measuring distances

Distance Measuring Equipment (DME) is also used on the busiest routes. A signal is sent from the plane to a station on the ground. When the signal is picked up by the ground beacon, it automatically sends off a reply

Over the Atlantic all planes within an air corridor must fly at the same speed.

air corridor at 33,000 feet (10,058 meters)

air corridor at 31,000 feet (9450 meters)

Right: An automatic pilot panel. The instrument can do anything a human pilot can—as long as it is given the right information.

signal to the airplane. The plane's DME system can work out the distance between the plane and the beacon by measuring the time interval between the plane's signal and the beacon's reply. A dial shows the distance in nautical miles.

Landing the airplane

When approaching an airport, the pilot uses Instrument Landing System (ILS) beams. These radio beams are sent out by devices on the ground and picked up by the plane's electronics. There are three beams. The marker beam from outer, middle and inner beacons shows how far the plane is from the runway. The glidepath beam gives the correct angle of descent.

The third beam is from the airport localizer beacon. The plane picks this up about 20 to 30 miles (30 to 50 kilometers) out and at about 2000 feet (610 meters). Various marker beacons tell the pilot how far he has gone as he approaches the airport. The glidepath signal is received next, when the plane is nearer the airport.

This leads the pilot in the proper direction and also at the proper angle down to the end of the runway.

Weather radar

Weather radar is used by airplanes to give the crew warning of bad weather conditions, so that they can avoid them. The equipment is a radar antenna in the front of the plane and a screen to show storm clouds in the ATMOSPHERE ahead. Weather can be seen as far away as 300 miles (480 kilometers). By pointing the radar downward it can also be used to show the main features of the ground.

Communications

Radio messages are sent by VHF (Very High Frequency) channels. At this frequency, radio signals travel only as far as the earth's horizon, so the range of VHF radio depends on how high the plane is flying. At the normal operating heights, this gives a limit of about 250 miles (400 kilometers).

The Inertial Navigation System (INS) is controlled by a small computer (below). It stores in its memory details of the flight plan and up to nine route changes. When it completes one section of the flight, it automatically changes course to the next section, giving the autopilot its instructions.

10 nautical miles (19 kilometers) wide

air corridor at 32,000 feet (9754 meters)

To prevent mid-air collisions, planes fly along air "corridors." Since some planes fly faster than others, the corridors are divided into speed zones. But instead of being side by side, these zones are one above the other.

Aircrews can also use world-wide radio communication in the 2 to 30 MHz (MegaHertz) band.

Normally a radio operator must listen all the time for incoming signals. But airplanes are now fitted with an automatic system. The radio receiver in the plane is left tuned to a certain frequency. Ground stations can send out a two-tone signal coded for whichever airplane they want. A buzzer or a flashing light tells the crew that someone is calling them.

We still need the pilot

Even with two sets of all this modern equipment for safety, there is still the pilot to fly the plane if both sets fail.

See also: ACCELEROMETER, AIRPLANES, AIRPORT, AIR TRAFFIC CONTROL, CLOUDS, FLIGHT RECORDER, FLIGHT SIMULATOR, GYROSCOPE, NAVIGATION, RADAR

Bacteria

Bacteria are the smallest and most simple forms of life. These tiny living cells are in the air we breathe, the food we eat and the water we drink. They can exist in the hottest and the coldest places on earth, at the bottom of the oceans and 20 miles (30 kilometers) up in the air. Some can be harmful, others we need for our very existence.

Useful bacteria

Although they are so small, bacteria (the singular is bacterium) are very important to human life. When a plant or animal dies, it is bacteria that break down the dead matter into simple chemicals that can be used by living things. We call this process decay or decomposition.

The process is most important in the soil, where bacteria make nitrogen from decaying matter. Other bacteria take nitrogen from the air and change it so that it can be used by plants. Green plants must have nitrogen to grow. And all animals depend on plant life.

Bacteria which live off dead or decaying matter are called SAPROPHYTES. Most bacteria are saprophytes.

People use bacteria in many ways. Some pleasant food flavors are created by the action of bacteria. Cheeses, some meats, cream and other foods are improved by ripening. This ripening is carried out by harmless bacteria. When we cook something or freeze

Below left: A photograph taken through a microscope shows tiny corkscrew-shaped bacteria (yellow).

Below: Bacteria have many different shapes. The most important are the *bacilli* (rod-shaped), *cocci* (ball-shaped), *vibrio* (curved) and *spirilla* (corkscrew-shaped). *Streptococci* can cause sore throats and make pus form in wounds. *Staphylococci* join together like bunches of grapes. They cause boils, abscesses and infection in wounds. *Streptomyces* are rod-shaped bacteria that join together. They are usually found in the soil.

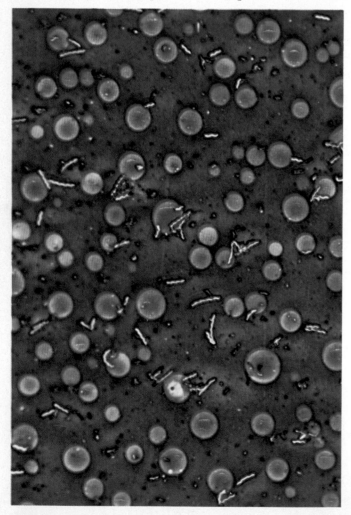

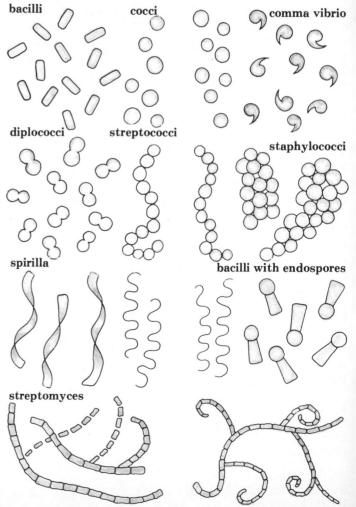

bacilli   cocci   comma vibrio

diplococci   streptococci   staphylococci

spirilla   bacilli with endospores

streptomyces

it, we stop the action of bacteria. But we must always remember that bacteria can only be killed by high temperatures. If we merely "warm" food we are probably making it easier for harmful bacteria to grow.

Harmful bacteria

Many bacteria cause diseases in people and animals. Tuberculosis, pneumonia, diphtheria, typhoid and whooping cough are among the diseases caused by these tiny living cells. They also cause various kinds of blood poisoning. We call harmful bacteria "germs."

Doctors can now cure many diseases by using antibiotics that stop harmful bacteria from growing. One of the best-known antibiotics is penicillin, a drug that was discovered in 1928 by Alexander Fleming. Since its discovery it has helped to save countless lives.

Doctors also prevent infectious diseases by injecting into our bodies some of the bacteria in a harmless form. These bacteria make our body prepare its defenses against the disease.

Different kinds of bacteria

Each tiny bacterium is a single living cell with a hard cell wall. Most of them are shaped like a short rod and are called *bacilli*. Others are long and curled or corkscrew-shaped—the *spirilla*. Still others are round balls and are called *cocci*. Sometimes bacteria change their shape, depending on where they grow.

Bacteria can move about by swimming or wriggling. Some have a swimming tail called a *flagellum* and hair-like *cilia* that push the bacteria through the liquids in which they swim.

How bacteria multiply

Bacteria multiply by splitting in half. There are no males and females. When a bacterium splits in two, each half is identical to the other. Most bacteria can reproduce very quickly, splitting in half every 20 minutes or so in good conditions. If one bacterium were to divide and divide again every 20 minutes, in only six hours there would be almost five million bacteria. In a single day there would be millions of tons of them. But this cannot happen because it would be impossible to keep them supplied with enough food.

As time goes by, doctors are learning a great deal about bacteria and how they work. The speed with which they grow and multiply is making them more and more useful in studying all kinds of medical problems.

We now know many ways of protecting ourselves against harmful bacteria. Many of them can be killed with drugs. But, above all, we now know how to handle and store food so that dangerous bacteria do not have a chance to live and multiply.

See also: ANTIBIOTICS, CELLS, PHOTOSYNTHESIS

Did you know?

Bacteria are so small that they can only be seen through a microscope. The period at the end of this sentence would cover about 1000 of them.

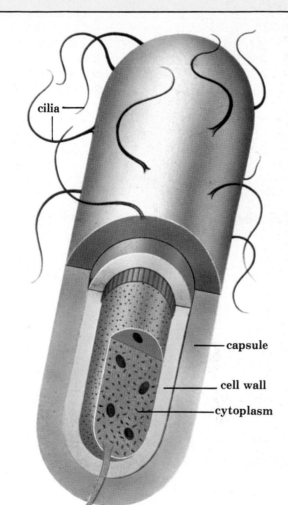

cilia

capsule

cell wall

cytoplasm

flagellum

Above: A typical bacterium. All the main life processes take place in the cytoplasm—the bacterium's factory. The *flagellum* and *cilia* are for moving the bacterium about. The cell wall is a tough layer that holds the bacterium together. Outside it, some bacteria have a slimy capsule covering that protects them from chemicals in which they swim.

Balances

The balance was one of man's first measuring instruments. It was probably invented by the ancient Egyptians or Babylonians around 5000 BC. It was first used for weighing gold. Today, similar balances are still in use to weigh precious metals, chemicals and various commercial goods.

Two-pan balance

The first balances were made of a simple beam, hinged at its center, and with a pan hanging at each end. The article to be weighed was placed in one pan, and weights were placed in the other pan until a balance was obtained. Modern two-pan balances work on the same principle, although various improvements have been made in the design.

One important improvement in the design of balances was made by the Romans. At the balance point, or FULCRUM, of the beam they fixed a triangular section on which it could rest. Balancing the beam on this "knife edge" made the instrument much more sensitive and accurate, especially when measuring light objects.

Where extreme accuracy is not necessary, a simple and strong balance can be used. But, for precision weighing, great care must be taken with design and construction in order to have fewer mistakes. The chemical balance used in science laboratories is often a highly accurate two-pan design.

Chemical balance

The chemical balance is mounted on a base with adjustable legs. These are screwed in or out until the base is horizontal, as shown on a built-in spirit level. The beam of the balance is made from a light, rigid alloy. At the center of the beam is an agate knife edge that acts as a pivot. This rests on an agate plate at the top of a central metal column.

The pans of the balance hang from devices called STIRRUPS. These are supported by agate plates resting on knife edges, one at each end of the beam. A man-made sapphire is sometimes used for the knife edges and plates instead of agate. These extremely hard materials are chosen in order to reduce wear and thus maintain high accuracy.

A long pointer, fixed to the center of the beam, extends down to a scale at the bottom of the column. When the pointer is in the middle of the scale, the beam is perfectly balanced.

Placing an object or weight on a hanging pan could damage the fine knife edges, so a mechanism is provided to lower the pans onto supports. To see if the object and weights balance, a knob is turned to raise the beam so that the pans hang freely.

A glass-sided case protects the instrument from air

Top: A chemical balance for weighing objects up to 7 ounces (200 grams). The weights are handled with forceps to avoid corrosion.

Bottom: A balance invented by de Roberval, a 17th century mathematician.

currents which might upset the delicate balance. The case also keeps out dirt and reduces CORROSION.

Single-pan balance

This balance has a pan and a set of weights suspended from one end of a pivoted beam. At the other end of the beam is a fixed counterweight. When there is nothing in the pan, the beam balances. So if an object is placed in the pan, one or more of the weights must be taken out to restore the balance. When a balance has been found, the sum of the removed weights is equal to the weight of the object in the pan.

The weights are moved by turning knobs on the outside of the case. The beam pointer is usually mounted near the counterweight. Its image is projected onto a scale at the front.

The single-pan balance is widely used in industrial, medical and research laboratories throughout the world. It has become more popular than the two-pan balance as it is much easier to use.

Damping

In single and two-pan balances, the pointer swings from side to side for a while before coming to rest. In sensitive balances, this could take a long time. So a technique called "damping" is used to bring the beam and pointer to rest quickly.

Pneumatic damping

The most common arrangement is known as pneumatic damping. One end of the beam moves a loose-fitting piston in a cylinder. When it moves, the piston forces air in or out of the cylinder. As one end of the cylinder is sealed, the piston has to force the air through the small gap between the piston and cylinder. This effort prevents the piston from moving quickly, and causes the beam to come gently to rest with little vibration.

See also: **CHEMISTRY**

Below: A typical single-pan balance as used today in laboratories throughout the world. Placing an object on the pan makes it move down. Removing some of the small weights restores the balance. The sum of the weights removed equals the weight of the object.

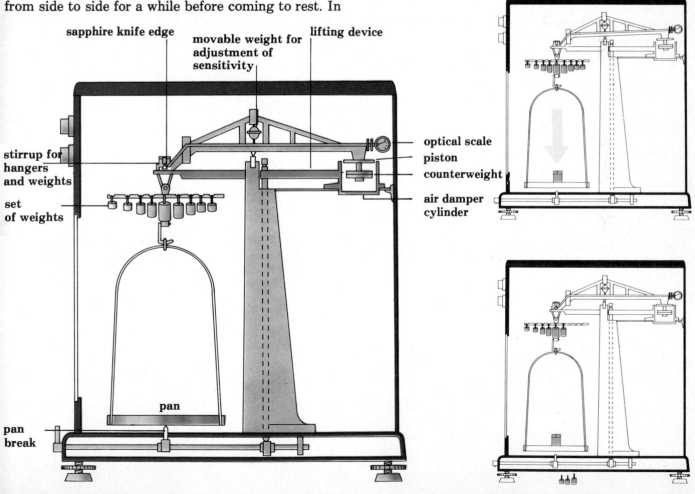

sapphire knife edge

movable weight for adjustment of sensitivity

lifting device

stirrup for hangers and weights

set of weights

optical scale
piston
counterweight

air damper cylinder

pan

pan break

Ballistics

Ballistics is a branch of science that deals with the movement of bullets, bombs, rockets and other projectiles. The three main branches of this science deal with the firing, flight and final damage of the projectile.

Interior ballistics

Interior ballistics deals with the firing of projectiles. In a gun, for example, a device called a firing pin strikes the bullet case, setting off an explosive powder. This produces gases that expand rapidly, forcing the bullet out of the gun barrel. Specialists in internal ballistics design guns and bullets according to the range and effect required.

Unlike a bullet, a rocket carries the fuel that propels it. The fuel continues burning after the rocket has been launched.

Exterior ballistics

Exterior ballistics is the study of a projectile's flight path. For a bullet, the path (trajectory) resembles a curve called a PARABOLA. Various forces affect the movement of the bullet. The earth's gravity makes it curve gradually toward the ground. If there is no obstacle in its path, the bullet will travel farthest when it is fired at an angle of about 45 degrees to the ground.

The air tends to resist the motion of the bullet and also to tilt its nose upward. As a result, the bullet slows down and tends to tumble. To prevent the tumbling motion, and keep the bullet pointing forward, it is usually given a twist as it leaves the gun. This is done by means of a spiral groove in the barrel. Like a gyroscope, the spinning bullet resists being tilted. In arrows and rockets, the problem is overcome by fitting tail fins. These increase the air resistance at the back so that the nose always stays in front.

The path of a rocket is controlled by the thrust of its engines. When the engines are switched off, the rocket may fall to the ground. But, under certain conditions, the rocket may orbit the earth, or even escape from it and head into outer space.

Terminal ballistics

Terminal ballistics is the study of damage done by missiles to their targets. The damage may be caused in various ways.

Bombs destroy their targets by explosion or fire. Bullets damage tissues by impact and penetration. High-speed bullets can pass right through the body, causing much damage at the entry and exit points.

Bullets like this are unsuitable for police fighting street crimes, for a bullet could pass through the criminal and hit an innocent person. Instead, low-speed bullets that spread out on impact are used. These lodge in the target.

See also: AMMUNITION, GYROSCOPE, ROCKETS

Below: Instead of leaving a neat hole, a high-speed bullet can severely damage a target. As shown here, the shock waves produced can destroy large areas of tissue around the points where the bullet enters and leaves its target. The study of such effects is called terminal ballistics.

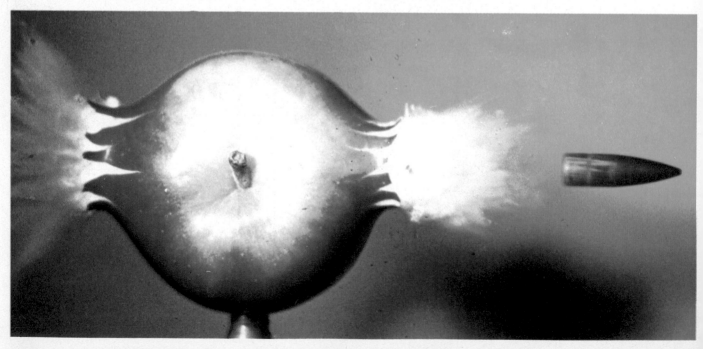

Balloons

Balloons are the one form of lighter-than-air craft that span the entire history of manned flight. They were the means by which man first took to the air in the 1700s. Today, they are widely used for various kinds of scientific research as well as for fun.

Ballooning history

The first manned flight took place on November 21, 1783, by means of a hot air balloon. Hot air is less dense than cool air and will rise. Therefore, a balloon filled with hot air will lift the balloon and its basket of passengers into the sky. The balloon used for man's first flight was made by the Montgolfier brothers, Joseph and Etienne, who were paper manufacturers.

Their balloon was a flimsy craft made from cloth backed with paper and measured 75 feet (23 meters) high by nearly 50 feet (15 meters) across. A furnace burning chopped straw heated the air. The pilots on this historic voyage were Pilatre de Rozier and the Marquis d'Arlandes. The balloon, launched in Paris, crossed the River Seine at a height of nearly 1000 feet (300 meters). It landed 25 minutes later just over 5 miles (8 kilometers) away.

The following month, the first ascent in a hydrogen-filled balloon took place, also in Paris. Hydrogen tends to rise even at normal temperatures, so the hydrogen balloon needs no heating. One problem of the first hot air balloons was that the fire that heated the air often charred or even set fire to the balloon's fabric. So the hydrogen balloon soon became regarded as superior. The first manned hydrogen balloon flight was made by Jacques Charles and M. N. Robert. Their balloon, made of silk coated with rubber to make it airtight, took them from Paris to the town of Nesles, about 27 miles (43 kilometers) away. These first flights started a craze for ballooning and led to the use of balloons for sporting, military and scientific uses.

Balloons at war

In the American Civil War, both armies used balloons as military lookout posts. These balloons were tied to the ground by means of long cables. From their position high above the ground, the observers could see enemy troops many miles away.

Balloons were also used for observation in World War I, although this job was gradually taken over by the early powered airplanes. The advantage of the airplane was that it could be steered. The balloon, if released, could only go where the wind took it.

Another military use of the balloon was for bombing. In 1849, the Austrians loaded paper hot air balloons with small bombs. The balloons were released so that they drifted toward Venice. And, as late as 1944, the Japanese released hydrogen balloons loaded with bombs in the direction of Canada and the United

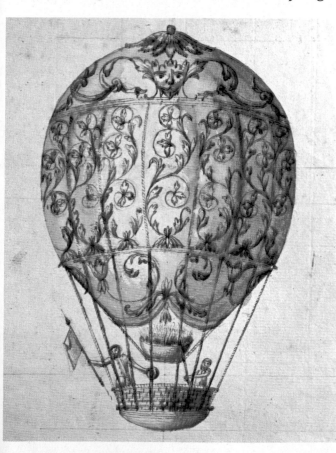

Above: A Caquot observation balloon, developed in World War I. Such balloons were also used widely in World War II.

Left: An 18th century hot air balloon heated by burning straw in a small furnace.

States. But again, being unable to guide the balloons made the technique unreliable.

From the 1850s, long, propeller-driven balloons called airships were developed. As these airships did not need to rely on wind direction, they proved of great use to the armed forces. Germany and Britain used airships during World War I for both observation and bombing raids. However, the ordinary balloon still had its uses.

In World War II, barrage balloons were used in Europe to protect ships and cities from air attack. Several of these balloons would be anchored in a line. The steel cables that held them in position were a serious danger to low-flying enemy aircraft.

Ballooning as a sport

The early balloons provided great sport for their brave pilots. And, once reliable balloons had been developed, numerous contests and races were organized. The best known were the Gordon Bennett races, which took place in Europe from 1906 to 1938. In this series, the greatest distance traveled by balloon was 1368 miles (2191 kilometers).

Ballooning died out as a sport with the outbreak of World War II in 1939. During and immediately after the war, gas-filled balloons were used by the armed forces. Then, in the mid-1950s, Ed Yost, working for the American company General Mills, revived interest in the hot air balloon. Using modern techniques, Yost felt sure that he could get better lift than with the early hot air balloons.

The United States Navy showed interest in the project and gave Yost a $47,000 grant to carry out research. Yost formed a new company called Raven Industries, and produced a successful hot air balloon. But, in 1963, the Navy lost interest in the project, so the company decided to market the design as a sporting balloon. Ballooning was revived as a sport and, today, Raven Industries is the world leader in balloon manufacture.

Scientific balloons

Unmanned gas-filled balloons are often used for weather observation and scientific research. Weather

Below: The gondola, the well-equipped living quarters for a round-the-world balloon trip. This capsule is made of aluminum and has solar heating.

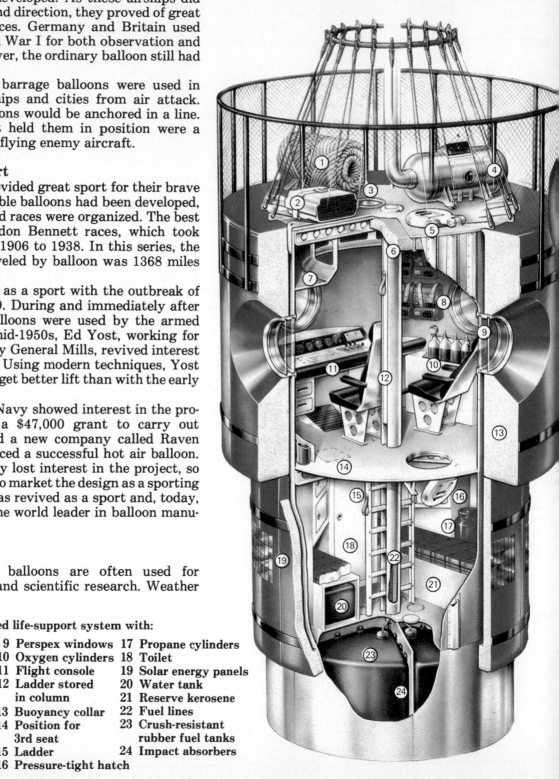

Gondola: A self-contained life-support system with:

1 Trail rope	9 Perspex windows	17 Propane cylinders
2 Life raft for four	10 Oxygen cylinders	18 Toilet
3 Viewing window	11 Flight console	19 Solar energy panels
4 Gas turbine heater and power generator	12 Ladder stored in column	20 Water tank
5 Pressure-tight hatch	13 Buoyancy collar	21 Reserve kerosene
6 Thermal insulation foam	14 Position for 3rd seat	22 Fuel lines
7 Storage space	15 Ladder	23 Crush-resistant rubber fuel tanks
8 Parachutes	16 Pressure-tight hatch	24 Impact absorbers

balloons carry instruments that measure temperature, pressure, humidity and other atmospheric conditions. The measurements can be sent back to the ground automatically by radio, or they can be recorded on charts by an instrument carried in the balloon.

In this case, scientists have to recover the instrument pack when the balloon returns to earth in order to obtain the information they require.

Circulating winds often carry weather balloons around the earth at a height of over 15 miles (24 kilometers). The instruments they carry weigh about 90 pounds (41 kilograms). Most weather balloons measure about 65 feet (20 meters) in diameter, but much larger versions are planned for carrying loads of up to 500 pounds (226 kilograms) to a height of 22 miles (35 kilometers).

Besides recording weather conditions, instruments in balloons can also measure pollution and RADIATION in the upper ATMOSPHERE, and detect the presence of METEORITES. In one scientific experiment, two balloons were used to lift instruments weighing 13,000 pounds (6000 kilograms).

Balloon flight principles

Heavier-than-air machines, such as gliders and airplanes, create a lifting force by moving through the air. This force holds them up. By contrast, a balloon is a lighter-than-air device. It moves with the air, not through it, and obtains its lifting force by means of DISPLACEMENT. This means that it displaces a volume of ordinary air and puts something lighter in its place, for example hydrogen gas or hot air.

Imagine what happens when a volume of still air in the atmosphere is displaced by the same volume of a lighter gas. If a volume of air is still, it must be because the air pressure below holds it up. When the volume of

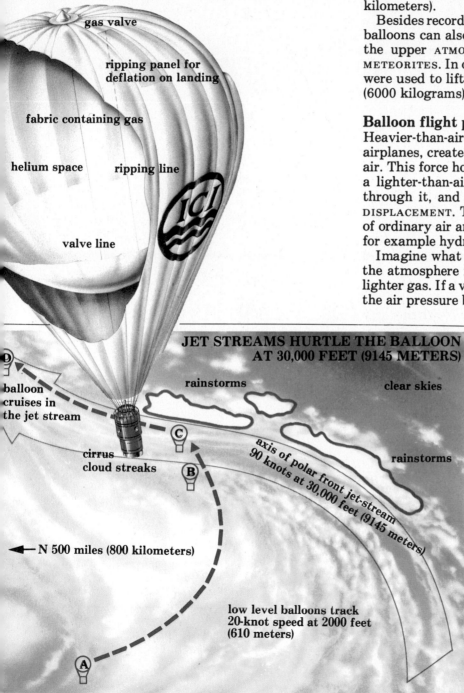

gas valve

ripping panel for deflation on landing

fabric containing gas

helium space

ripping line

valve line

JET STREAMS HURTLE THE BALLOON AT 30,000 FEET (9145 METERS)

rainstorms

clear skies

balloon cruises in the jet stream

cirrus cloud streaks

rainstorms

axis of polar front jet-stream 90 knots at 30,000 feet (9145 meters)

← N 500 miles (800 kilometers)

low level balloons track 20-knot speed at 2000 feet (610 meters)

Left: The balloon designed for the first proposed round-the-world trip was named *Innovation*. It measured 200 feet (61 meters) high and would use both helium and hot air in order to obtain the necessary lift. In the day, sunlight would warm the helium gas so that it expands to fill the envelope. At night, the turbine generator would pump hot air into the bottom of the balloon. The balloon was designed to cruise in the jet streams. These fast-moving winds cross the globe at high altitudes. By making use of these winds, it was hoped that the complete trip around the world would last only 20 days.

air is displaced by a lighter gas, the air pressure below remains the same. But now it has a lighter gas to support, so the air pressure is sufficient to force the volume of gas upward. If the gas is contained in a balloon, the whole structure will be pushed up into the sky. This happens provided that the balloon skin and the load carried are not too heavy.

A balloon is said to be in EQUILIBRIUM in the air when it remains balanced at the same height. Its total weight is then the same as the weight of the air that it displaces. The pressure that would have supported the air is, therefore, just enough to support the balloon instead. This is why the balloon remains at the same height instead of moving up or down.

The lifting force of a balloon depends on the gas filling it. At sea level, 1000 cubic feet (28 cubic meters) of hot air at 212 degrees F (100 degrees C) can lift a load of 17 pounds (8 kilograms) when the surrounding air is at 60 degrees F (16 degrees C). A similar volume of hydrogen would lift 70 pounds (32 kilograms). Helium, another gas used in balloons, would lift a load of 65 pounds (30 kilograms).

For the greatest amount of lift, hydrogen is obviously the best gas to use in balloons. But cost, convenience and safety are also important. Today, hydrogen, helium and hot air balloons all have their different uses.

Gas balloons

Gas balloons are filled with hydrogen or helium. Hot air balloons are not called gas balloons, even though air is a mixture of gases. Most gas balloons are filled with hydrogen, which is extremely light. But great care must be taken as it catches on fire easily and forms an explosive mixture when combined with air. Helium is safe as it does not burn, and it produces almost as much lift as hydrogen. But it is much more expensive than hydrogen in most countries, except the United States.

Modern gas balloons for manned flight have a round envelope made from fabric sealed with rubber or neoprene. Around the envelope is a thin rope net with a horizontal ring hanging from it. A basket carrying the crew and equipment is hung from this ring.

As a balloon goes up, the surrounding air pressure gradually decreases. As a result, the gas in the balloon is able to expand. To prevent the balloon from bursting, a gas escape tube is provided at the bottom of the envelope. This tube, called the APPENDIX, acts as a valve. It allows some gas to escape, but prevents the entry of air into the envelope. A gas balloon is made to rise by throwing sand bags or other heavy objects from the basket. To come down, gas is let out through a small valve in the top of the envelope. The valve is operated by a cord leading down into the basket.

Hot air balloons

Modern hot air balloons are cheaper, easier to operate

Above: In 1978, *Double Eagle II* became the first balloon to cross the Atlantic.

and safer than gas balloons. The envelope, tapering toward the bottom, is usually made from nylon material. Nylon tapes sewn to the envelope support the basket and a gas burner that heats the air. Modern burners use propane gas, blowing the hot air up into an opening in the bottom of the envelope. The balloon is made to go up by turning on the burner to heat the air. Turning off the burner allows the air to cool again, so that the balloon goes down toward the ground.

Hot air balloons of the future may be kept in the air by heat from the sun.

See also: AIRSHIPS, BOMBS, WEATHER FORECASTING

Ballpoint Pen

The ballpoint pen has a tiny steel ball at its tip. When the pen is being used, the ball rotates, automatically coating itself with ink. This is stored in a reservoir tube inside the body of the pen. The ink is too thick to leak out accidentally.

Invention and improvement
The American John Loud invented the ballpoint pen in 1888. Although it was much larger than today's slim ballpoint pens, Loud's model worked the same way. Loud used his pen for marking leather and fabrics, but it was never manufactured in large quantities.

In 1938, the Hungarian brothers László and Georg Biró patented a more reliable ballpoint pen. The following year, working from Argentina, they gave permission to companies in other countries to produce the pens. They were soon widely used in Britain, and became commonly known as "biros."

In the United States, ballpoint pens became popular after they had been accepted for use by the armed forces in 1942.

Modern designs
Although the ball of the pen is usually made of steel, other hard substances, such as sapphire or tungsten carbide are sometimes used. The ball, usually 1/25 inch (1 millimeter) in DIAMETER, is held in a socket. The back of the socket leads to a metal or plastic tube containing the ink. As the ink in the socket is used up, it is replaced by ink flowing down from the reservoir tube.

Early ballpoint pens sometimes leaked because the printer's ink they used was too runny. Modern ballpoint pens contain a thicker ink made from a dye dissolved in oil or spirit. The oil-based ink dries quickly by being ABSORBED into the writing surface. Spirit-based ink dries by EVAPORATION and tends to give sharper lines.

In order for the ink to flow properly, an opening must be provided at the far end of the tube. If the tube is narrow, it can be left completely open. The thickness of the ink prevents it from leaking through the narrow opening. Some reservoir tubes are quite wide so that they can hold more ink. In such cases, the end of the tube has a plug with a small hole through it.

Above the ink is a layer of an even thicker liquid called a follower. This is thick enough not to leak out, but is just runny enough to follow the ink down the tube as the pen is used. When the ink runs out, the ball and reservoir unit are normally replaced with a refill. In many pens, a spring mechanism allows the point to be drawn into the pen body after use.

Right: A cross-section through a ballpoint pen. Only its tip is made of metal.

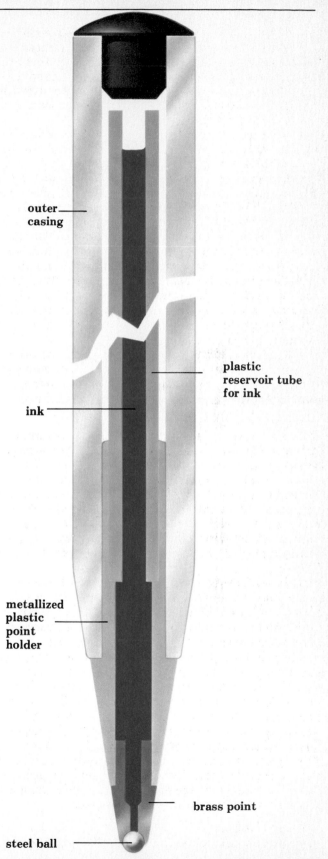

outer casing

plastic reservoir tube for ink

ink

metallized plastic point holder

brass point

steel ball

Barometers

The barometer is an invention which has made it possible to forecast any changes in the weather. It is used to measure the pressure of the air. The level of mercury in a tube will fall (low pressure) for bad weather and rise (high pressure) if good weather is on the way.

Mercury barometers

The air pressure on any part of the earth is caused by the column of air above it. At sea level, this pressure is about 15 pounds per square inch.

A common way of measuring air pressure is to use it to support a column of liquid in a glass tube. The greater the air pressure, the higher the column of liquid that it will support. Mercury is the liquid most often used in barometers. Normal atmospheric (air) pressure will support a mercury column about 30 inches (76 centimeters) high. For this reason, normal atmospheric pressure is often referred to as a pressure of 30 inches (76 centimeters) of mercury.

Other liquids can be used in barometers instead of mercury, but the main advantage of mercury is that it is extremely dense. A given volume of it weighs 13.6 times as much as the same volume of water. So a relatively short column of mercury is enough to balance the pressure of the atmosphere. If water was used, the

column would have to be 13.6 times as long—34 feet (10 meters) instead of 30 inches (76 centimeters).

Another advantage of mercury is that it freezes at a much lower temperature than water. So the mercury barometer will keep working even in icy conditions.

Torricelli's barometer

The Italian scientist Galileo was the first to show that the atmosphere has weight and exerts pressure. But it was Galileo's pupil Torricelli who worked out the principle of the barometer in 1643.

Below: In the mercury barometer (1), air pressure pushes down on the mercury in the container. This pressure supports the column of mercury in the tube. In this case, the low pressure supports a column 28 inches high. If the pressure increases (2), the column height increases. Here, the scale shows a reading of 30 inches. But this is not correct, as the lower mercury level has moved down. To overcome this problem, Torricelli's barometer (3) has a scale that can be moved to line up its zero mark with the lower mercury level. The scale then shows a true pressure reading of 31 inches. In the Fortin barometer (4), the container is moved in order to line up the mercury level with the zero mark on the scale. Again, a true pressure reading of 31 inches is obtained.

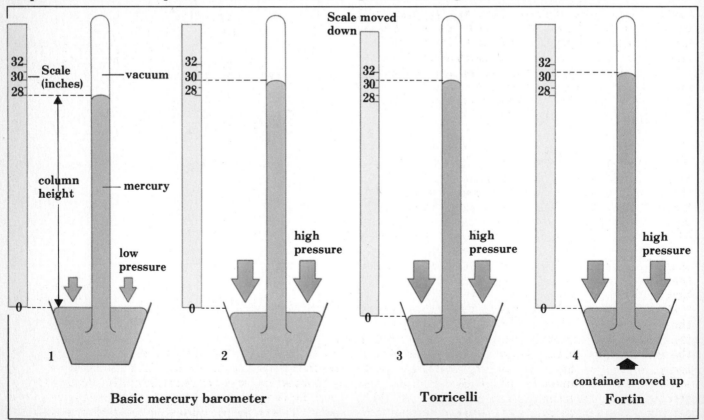

Basic mercury barometer   Torricelli   Fortin

Torricelli filled a long glass tube with mercury and placed the lower end in an open dish of the liquid. The mercury level in the tube dropped until it was about 30 inches (76 centimeters) above the level in the dish. The space left in the sealed top of the tube contained nothing but a little mercury VAPOR at low pressure. This space is sometimes called a Torricellian vacuum.

In Torricelli's mercury barometer, the air pressure on the mercury in the dish held the mercury column up in the tube. Any change in air pressure would, therefore, cause a corresponding change in the height of the column. So measuring the mercury column gave an indication of the air pressure. However, measuring the height of the column was not quite so simple.

One way to measure the height of the mercury column is to use a ruler fixed to the tube. The zero mark on the ruler should be lined up with the mercury level in the dish. The height can then be measured simply by noting the reading on the ruler opposite the top of the mercury column. However, any change in the air pressure will change the level of the mercury in the tube *and* in the dish.

For example, a pressure increase will push the level in the dish down, so that the level in the tube rises. And a pressure decrease will allow the level in the dish to rise, so that the level in the tube falls. The height we need to measure is from the level in the dish to the level in the tube. So, as the level in the tube changes, we must move the ruler up or down so that its zero mark is once again lined up with the level in the dish. Only then will the reading on the ruler be a true measure of the height.

Having to reset the scale before taking a reading was not very convenient. But this problem was overcome in later versions of the mercury barometer: the Fortin and Kew designs.

Fortin barometer

In the Fortin barometer, a scale is fixed to the tube, and the lower mercury level is adjusted to a zero mark before taking a reading. The mercury container, or cistern, at the bottom consists of a flexible leather bag. This rests on a large adjusting screw. Turning the screw raises or lowers the bottom of the cistern, which changes the mercury level. The screw is adjusted until the mercury just touches an ivory pointer fixed in position above the surface.

A clear reflection of the white pointer can be seen in the silvery surface of the mercury. So any gap between the pointer and mercury is shown up by a gap double the size between the pointer and its reflection. And, if the pointer is slightly submerged, its tip cannot be seen. This arrangement therefore allows an accurate setting of the mercury level to be obtained easily. After setting the lower mercury level, the column height is measured on the fixed scale.

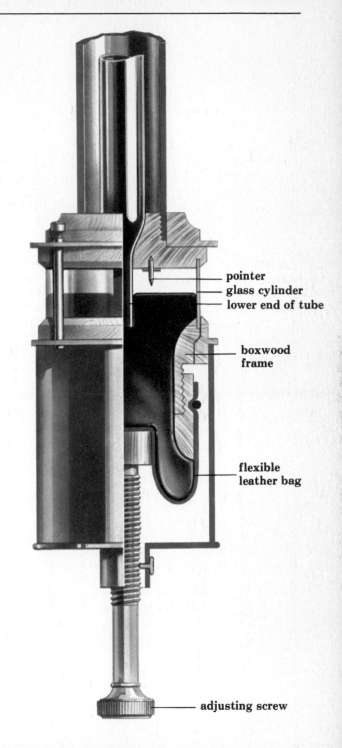

pointer
glass cylinder
lower end of tube

boxwood frame

flexible leather bag

adjusting screw

Above: The Fortin barometer was designed by Jean Fortin in the early 1800s. Before taking a reading, the mercury level in the glass cylinder must be set so that it just touches the pointer. This is done by turning the large screw to move the leather bag up or down. The pressure can then be read from a scale fixed to the glass tube.

Kew barometer

The Kew barometer is a mercury type that needs no zero adjustment. Its rigid cistern, usually made from iron or steel, has parallel sides. So the level of mercury

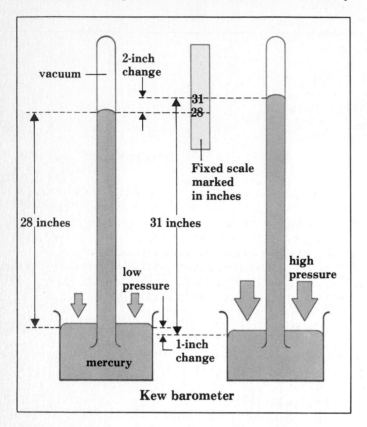

Kew barometer

Above: The diagrams show the basic operation of a Kew barometer. A fixed scale shows the air pressure in inches of mercury. In the example shown here, the pressure changes from 28 inches to 31 inches. This increase causes the lower level to fall by one inch. And the mercury in the tube is forced up by two inches. So, as expected, the column height increases by three inches—from 28 inches to 31 inches. The scale gives a reading or pressure with no need for any adjustment of the barometer. This is achieved by using a special scale instead of an ordinary ruler. In our example, the two-inch movement of the mercury in the tube shows on the scale the actual pressure change of three inches—from 28 to 31 inches. In other words, the marks on the scale are contracted, or squashed up compared with the marks on an ordinary ruler. For clarity, the amount of contraction has been exaggerated here.

Right: Unlike other mercury barometers, the Kew type needs no adjustment before taking a reading. The air trap prevents any air bubbles from reaching the top of the tube.

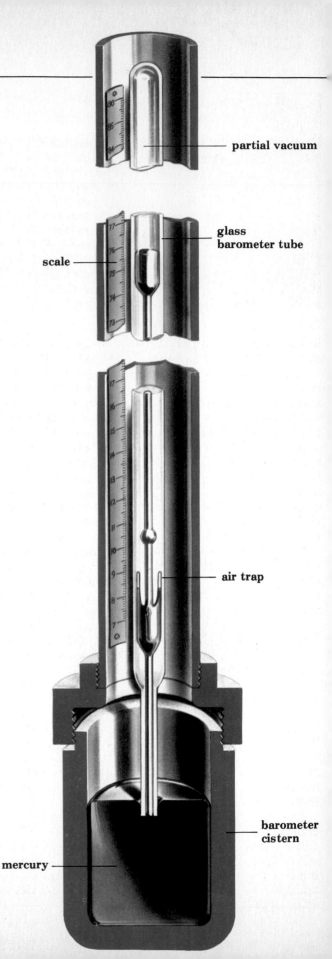

Left: An aneroid barometer made around 1876 in Hamburg.

Right: The aneroid barometer contains a corrugated metal vacuum capsule. Any change in the air pressure on the outside of this chamber causes its sides to move in or out. A mechanism transmits this movement to the pointer, which indicates the air pressure on a dial. Barometers of this kind are used in weather balloons and rockets.

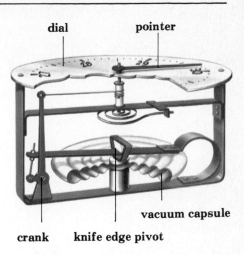

in the cistern always changes by the same amount for each inch that the mercury column rises or falls.

Suppose, for example, that a change in air pressure causes the mercury to rise by one inch in the tube. As mercury is drawn up from the cistern, the level there will fall slightly. So the height of the column, measured to the surface in the cistern, will have increased by just over one inch. For a height change of exactly one inch, therefore, the mercury in the tube would move a little less than this distance. So the fixed scale used to determine the column height has to be compressed. The distance between each inch mark on the scale is only slightly less than a true inch, the difference rarely being more than 5 percent.

If the barometer is shaken, air bubbles could enter the tube. It is important to stop the air from reaching the top of the tube as it would push the mercury down slightly and cause inaccurate readings. This is why the tube has an air trap to catch rising bubbles.

Kew barometers are usually designed to be portable. They have to be tilted carefully so that the mercury fills the glass tube. Then they can be carried upside down without risk of spilling the mercury.

Aneroid barometer

The Italian scientist Lucius Vidi invented the aneroid barometer in 1843. The term "aneroid" means without liquid. Although the aneroid barometer is not so sensitive or accurate as the mercury type, it is extremely strong. As there is no mercury to spill, the aneroid barometer is particularly suitable as a portable instrument.

The aneroid barometer contains a sealed metal chamber from which the air has been removed. This is called the bellows or vacuum capsule. It is disc shaped with flexible corrugated (grooved) sides. The surrounding air pushes on the sides of the capsule, which are held apart by a steel spring. So the separation between the sides depends on the pressure of the air.

As the air pressure changes, the sides of the capsule move in or out. This movement is extremely small, but it is magnified by a system of levers. The final lever moves a wire or fine chain wound around a spindle, making it turn against the force of a weak coiled spring. A pointer on the end of the spindle indicates the air pressure on a circular scale. Being cheap to produce, aneroid barometers are popular for home use.

The aneroid altimeter

An altimeter is an instrument used in aircraft. It measures the altitude, or height, of the aircraft above the ground. The aneroid altimeter works like an aneroid barometer. It measures the air pressure around it in order to find out the altitude.

High above the earth, the air is thin and exerts little pressure. So a low-pressure reading would mean that the aircraft is flying high. Lower down, the air pressure is greater. Hence a high-pressure reading would mean that the aircraft is near to the ground. To make the altimeter easy to use, its scale is marked in height instead of pressure.

Before use, the altimeter must be adjusted according to the air pressure at ground level. This reading is obtained by radio from a nearby weather station or airfield. The pressure at ground level is made to give a zero reading on the height scale. The instrument will then show the correct altitude of the aircraft.

A major problem with this type of altimeter is that the pilot may forget to adjust it before taking a reading. Any indication of height on the altimeter is really an indication of a low air pressure, which may be due to the aircraft's height. But it may instead be due to a general decrease in the air pressure in the region. In modern airliners, this problem does not arise. Altimeters now work by radar, not by measuring air pressure.

See also: AIR PRESSURE, RADAR, WEATHER FORECASTING

Bathyscaphe

Air tanks flood with water to dive.

Powered by an electric motor, the bathyscaphe moves slowly backward and forward when submerged.

Sea water flows in and out of these holes depending on how deep the bathyscaphe is in the water.

Tanks filled with gasoline.

These tanks are filled with tiny iron pellets. An electromagnet surrounds each tank.

Until 50 years ago, it was impossible to see exactly what the bottom of the ocean looked like, or to study the creatures living deep underwater. This was because there was no equipment which allowed divers to go down deep enough.

The development of the aqualung (SCUBA—short for Self-Contained Underwater Breathing Apparatus) did mean that a diver could go down about 165 feet (50 meters), but in oceanic terms this was not really very far. What was needed was a vessel to carry men deeper into the sea. The first such underwater ship was built by two Americans, William Beebe (a marine zoologist) and Otis Barton (an engineer). They called their vessel a

When the electromagnet is switched off, the iron pellets are released and fall into the sea.

The entrance tube, which can be sealed off from the cabin by closing the hatch, floods for diving. When the crew wants to leave, compressed air pushes the water out.

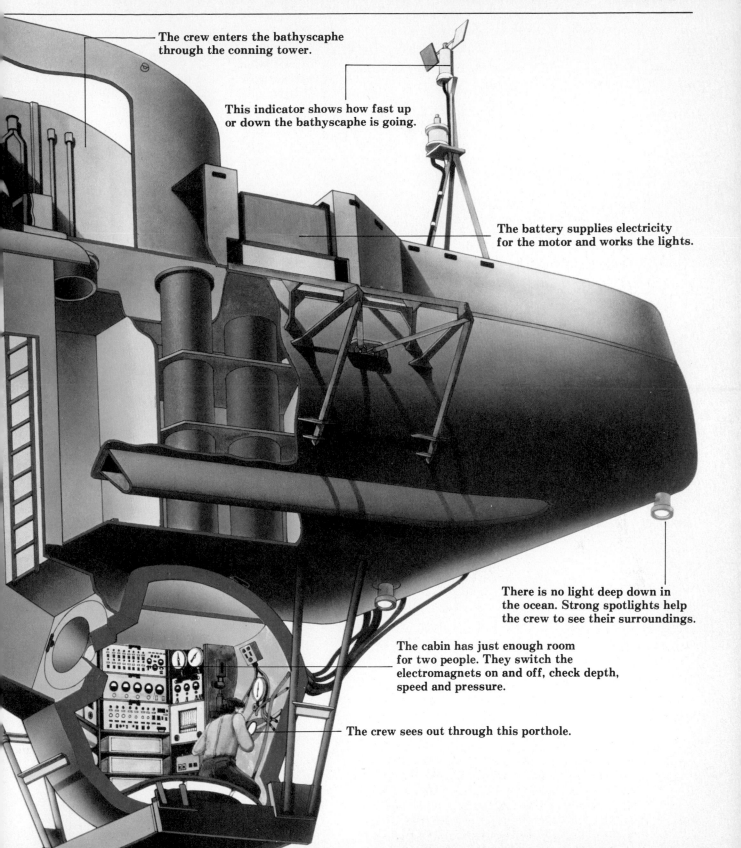

The crew enters the bathyscaphe through the conning tower.

This indicator shows how fast up or down the bathyscaphe is going.

The battery supplies electricity for the motor and works the lights.

There is no light deep down in the ocean. Strong spotlights help the crew to see their surroundings.

The cabin has just enough room for two people. They switch the electromagnets on and off, check depth, speed and pressure.

The crew sees out through this porthole.

bathysphere from the Greek word "bathys" meaning deep and "sphere" because of its rounded shape.

The bathysphere
From 1930 to 1934 Beebe and Barton carried out a series of dives in the Caribbean Sea, including a record-breaking one of 3028 feet (923 meters). They became the first human beings to see that the underwater world below 1000 feet (300 meters) really is completely black.

Their bathysphere was made of steel and was only 5 feet (1.5 meters) in DIAMETER. It was shaped like a ball—the best design for standing up to the tremendous outside pressure of the water. The vessel contained oxygen cylinders which the men used to control their own breathing supply. It also had three tiny portholes made from thick quartz.

It had to be lowered on a steel cable from a ship on the surface. There was a telephone link, too, so that Beebe and Barton could keep in touch with the surface. But the bathysphere had several disadvantages: because of the cable link it could not move around, and it could not go down as deep as the scientists would have liked. In rough seas there were dangerous stresses in the supporting cable.

Then came the bathyscaphe
A few years later, Professor Auguste Piccard, a Swiss physicist and high-altitude balloonist, designed the bathyscaphe. The name this time came from the Greek "bathys" meaning deep and "scaphos" meaning ship. It was simply a crew sphere, just like the bathysphere, hanging from a massive float. But it could go even deeper and did not need to be tied to a ship on the surface. It was driven by two small screw propellers, worked by battery-powered motors.

Design of the vessel
The bathyscaphe was a high-quality steel sphere with

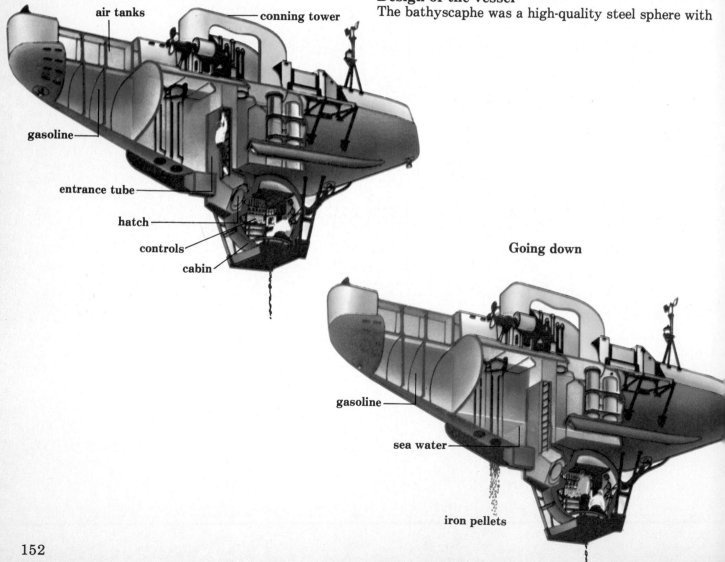

Getting ready

air tanks
conning tower
gasoline
entrance tube
hatch
controls
cabin

Going down

gasoline
sea water
iron pellets

an inside diameter of 6½ feet (2 meters). The steel walls were 3½ inches (9 centimeters) thick, strengthened to 6 inches (15 centimeters) around the portholes and door. The portholes had to be tremendously strong and perfectly sealed to the surrounding metal. This can create a problem because the pressures deep down in the ocean are so great that if just a few drops of water should seep through, they would soon become a strong and dangerous jet. To avoid this happening, the transparent plexiglass port was constructed like a cone with the narrow end sliced off. The cone was then placed, narrow end inwards, into a matching hole in the steel hull. This meant that as the pressure of water increased during the dive it pushed the port more securely into the hole in the hull.

The cabin had a system for renewing the air continually. This allowed the passengers to breathe normal, purified air at all times.

Operating the bathyscaphe

The top part of the bathyscaphe was a large metal float,

shaped like a ship's hull. This float was divided into compartments, some filled with gasoline, others with air. As gasoline is lighter than water, it gave the craft buoyancy.

Once the crew were aboard, the air tanks and the entrance tube flooded with sea water. This made the bathyscaphe heavier and it sank beneath the waves.

As the vessel continued its descent, sea water entered the gasoline tanks. This kept the pressure inside the float the same as the water pressure outside and stopped the outside pressure from crushing the float like a paper bag.

As the bathyscaphe went deeper, the sea water became colder and chilled the gas in the tanks. The cold made the gas contract, so more sea water entered the float. The bathyscaphe became heavier and heavier, and began to dive faster. To slow the dive down the

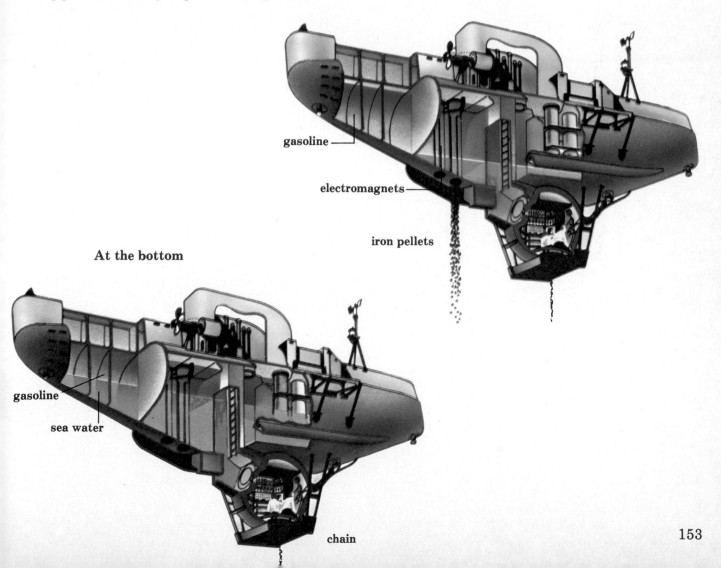

Coming up

gasoline

electromagnets

iron pellets

At the bottom

gasoline

sea water

chain

crew released some iron pellets which were carried as ballast. Several tons of these tiny metal balls were stored in two special containers under the float. They were held in place by ELECTROMAGNETS, powerful magnets operated by sending electric current through coils of wire. To release some iron pellets, the crew had merely to cut off the electric current for a few seconds and pellets fell to the seabed. This system ensured that the crew had very accurate control over their ballast system. It also meant that any accidental cutting off of the electricity supply would send the bathyscaphe to the surface.

Beneath the cabin of the bathyscaphe hung a length of heavy chain. When the vessel was nearing the seabed, the chain touched the bottom first. The vessel became lighter because some of the heavy chain was resting on the seabed. The bathyscaphe then hovered above the bottom and carried out its research.

The steel sphere held two men with enough air for about 24 hours. In addition to the controls for raising and lowering the craft, there were mechanical arms and a probe to test whether the seabed was solid or not. Powerful lights were needed to split the total darkness of the undersea world. Cameras and sonar equipment were also carried.

Above: The American *Alvin* underwater research vehicle. This vessel helped to salvage a hydrogen bomb which was lost in 1966.

The history of the bathyscaphe

The bathyscaphe was first tested off the coast of West Africa in 1948. Professor Piccard went down to a depth of over 2 miles (3 kilometers) in a second version of the craft called the *Trieste*. The United States Navy took over the bathyscaphe in 1958 and it was taken to California. A new cabin was fitted. On January 23, 1960, Dr. Jacques Piccard, the inventor's son, and Lt. Donald Walsh of the U.S. Navy descended into the Marianas Trench in the Pacific Ocean. They reached a depth of 35,802 feet (10,912 meters), a world record which still stands. Mount Everest, the world's highest moutain, is only about 29,000 feet (8,839 meters). The pressure at this depth was 1100 times greater than that of our ATMOSPHERE.

In 1979 the *Alvin* (above) returned from diving in the Galapagos Rift with the discovery of a new underwater creature.

See also: AQUALUNG, ELECTRIC CURRENT, SONAR

Battery

Batteries produce electricity by means of a chemical reaction. They are used wherever a portable supply of electrical power is needed. Pocket calculators, flashlights and automatic cameras are all battery-operated.

An electric cell is a device that produces electricity by means of a chemical reaction. Each type of cell produces a certain electrical force, or VOLTAGE. A battery consists of a number of cells connected together, usually to increase the voltage produced.

Invention of the battery

Experiments with electricity were carried out long before cells and batteries were invented. Some scientists experimented with electricity generated by friction (rubbing) machines. Others gathered the electricity released in thunderstorms.

In 1896, an Italian called Luigi Galvani prepared to experiment using dead frogs. A thunderstorm was approaching, and Galvani wanted to see what effect the electricity in the air would have on the frogs. While setting up the experiment, he found, to his astonishment, that the frogs' legs twitched whenever they touched two different metals.

Galvani realized that electricity caused the frogs to move, but was unaware of the importance of what he had done. He had, accidentally, produced a small, but fairly steady supply of electricity. In other words, Galvani had made a simple form of electric cell.

In the 1790s, another Italian, Alessandro Volta, explained the principle of the electric cell. Electricity could be produced by a combination of two different metals and a solution that would conduct (pass) electricity. In Galvani's experiment, the frogs' bodies had provided the necessary moisture. But Volta showed that a salt solution worked even better.

Using one copper disc and one of zinc, separated by a piece of cloth soaked in the solution, Volta made the first efficient electric cell. This produced only a small voltage. However, Volta found that this could be increased by stacking several cells to form a pile. Volta's pile formed the first battery. This was a most important invention, as it provided scientists with a steady flow of electricity (current). The battery was a store of electricity, which could be drawn off as required. Devices called capacitors, or CONDENSERS, had been used to store electricity produced by friction.

Right: A "dry" cell is not really dry, but its liquid chemicals cannot be spilt. Most of the cell is filled with a moist paste consisting of a mixture of chemicals. The electrolyte solution is held in a layer of absorbent paper. Dry cells are primary cells—they cannot be recharged.

But capacitors quickly discharge, the current falling rapidly to zero. Batteries, therefore, made it much easier for scientists to study electricity.

How cells work

Since Volta's time, many types of electric cell have been invented. But the basic principle of operation is the same in each case. An electric current (a flow of charged particles called ELECTRONS) is made to flow between two plates called ELECTRODES. Separating the electrodes is a chemical solution called the ELECTROLYTE. When the two plates are connected together by a wire a CIRCUIT is formed. This is the name for a completed path around which electricity passes.

Completion of the electrical circuit causes chemical reactions to take place at the electrodes of the cell. At one electrode, the reactions cause too many electrons to be produced. These electrons flow out of the cell, around the circuit, and back into the cell via the other electrode. Electrons have a negative electric charge, so the electrode from which they flow is called the negative electrode. The other electrode is called the positive electrode.

When a cell is in use, the chemical reactions that take

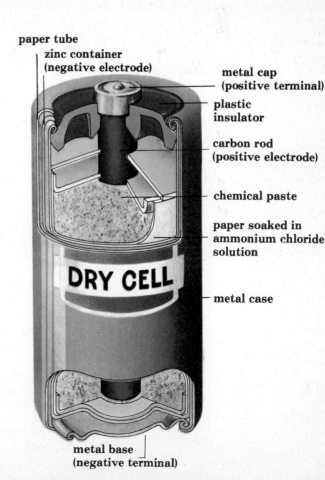

paper tube
zinc container (negative electrode)
metal cap (positive terminal)
plastic insulator
carbon rod (positive electrode)
chemical paste
paper soaked in ammonium chloride solution

DRY CELL

metal case

metal base (negative terminal)

place gradually change the electrolyte. Eventually, the cell "runs out" and can no longer supply current.

Primary and secondary cells

Most cells have to be replaced when they have run down. Cells of this type are called primary cells. The batteries commonly used in flashlights and portable radios contain primary cells. Other cells can be used again after recharging with electricity. These are called secondary cells, accumulators or storage cells.

Storage cells are recharged by connecting them to a charger. This is powered by the house electricity supply, and produces a suitable source for recharging the cells. Recharging, which takes several hours, reverses the chemical reactions that took place when the cells were in use. As a result, the electrolyte is gradually restored to its original state. When this process has been completed, the cells are ready for use once more.

A typical automobile battery has six storage cells connected together. An electricity generator, turned by the automobile engine, normally keeps the battery well charged. But if the engine is not running and the lights are left on for a long period, the battery will run down. It will then have to be connected to a battery charger to restore it to working order.

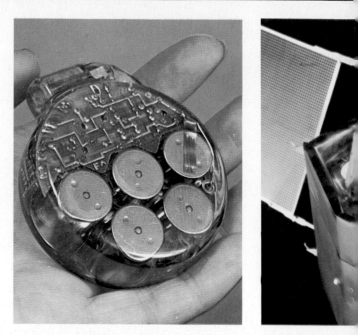

Above: The rate at which a faulty heart pumps blood can be regulated by an electronic pacemaker. The pacemaker shown here is powered by five tiny, long-life mercury cells.

Left: A storage battery contains secondary cells. These can be recharged with electricity after they have run down.

Below: In the fuel cell shown here, electricity is generated when the oxygen and hydrogen fuel react with potassium hydroxide.

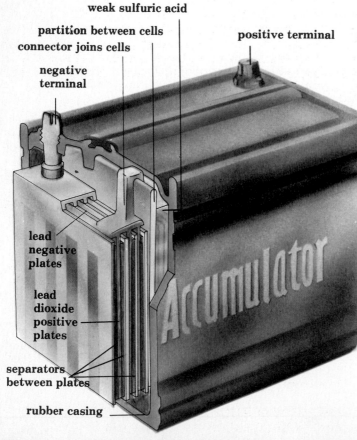

weak sulfuric acid

partition between cells
connector joins cells

negative terminal

positive terminal

lead negative plates

lead dioxide positive plates

separators between plates

rubber casing

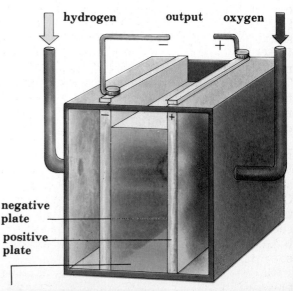

hydrogen   output   oxygen

negative plate

positive plate

potassium hydroxide solution

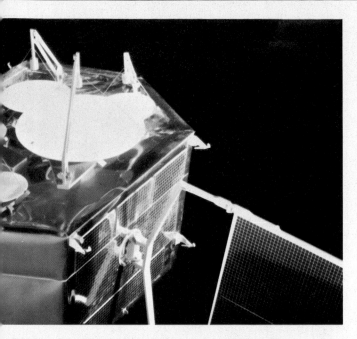

Above: A model of the European Orbital Test Satellite. The two wing-like structures are made up of solar panels. These are special batteries containing numerous tiny photoelectric cells. The cells convert the energy of sunlight into electricity, which is used to power the satellite's equipment. The solar panels are mounted on frames that automatically turn toward the sun. This ensures that the photoelectric cells receive maximum sunlight so that they can provide adequate electrical power.

The simple cell

The simple cell is a primary cell using one copper and one zinc electrode standing in a weak solution of sulfuric acid. Another name for sulfuric acid is hydrogen sulfate. The acid, which has the chemical formula H_2SO_4, acts as the electrolyte. In water, each acid molecule splits into three charged particles called IONS. The hydrogen (H) and one sulfate (SO_4) ions are formed from each acid molecule. The hydrogen ions each have a negative charge, and the sulfate ion has two positive charges.

Flow of electrons

When the cell is not in use, the zinc electrode has a slight negative charge—that is, an excess of electrons. On connecting a wire between the electrodes, the electrons flow as a current to the copper electrode. In the cell, zinc ions enter the solution. These leave electrons behind on the zinc plate, so the flow of electrons to the copper plate is maintained.

The zinc ions, having lost electrons (negative), are positively charged. Opposite charges attract. So the zinc ions attract the negative sulfate ions in the solution. A chemical reaction then takes place in which the zinc and sulfate particles combine to form zinc sulfate.

The electrons that travel to the copper plate attract the positively charged hydrogen ions in the solution. Each hydrogen atom receives one electron to form a normal, uncharged atom of hydrogen. The hydrogen atoms then join in pairs to form molecules of hydrogen gas. This can be seen bubbling to the surface of the solution.

The following equation sums up the chemical reactions that take place in the cell when it is supplying an electric current:

$$Zn + H_2SO_4 = ZnSO_4 + H_2$$
zinc   sulfuric   zinc   hydrogen
acid   sulfate

Problems with cells

Unless precautions are taken, cells suffer from side effects that limit their action or shorten their life. In the simple cell, for example, the zinc must be extremely pure. Most zinc contains iron as an impurity. In the acid, this would react with the zinc plate and cause it to be eaten away. This effect is called LOCAL ACTION.

Another problem encountered in cells is POLARIZATION. It is usually caused by gas formed at one of the electrodes. In the simple cell, some of the hydrogen bubbles formed at the copper plate remain there. After a while, a layer of bubbles covers the plate and prevents the cell from working properly. Modern cells are carefully designed to reduce local action and polarization to a minimum.

Modern cells and batteries

Dry cells are so named because they contain no free liquid. A zinc case acts as the negative electrode, and the electrolyte is ammonium chloride solution. This is contained in a layer of absorbent paper. A central carbon rod acts as the positive electrode. Most of the cell is filled with a chemical paste that reduces polarization.

Rechargeable nickel-cadmium cells have replaced dry cells in many items of portable electrical equipment. Although they cost more, they can be recharged extremely cheaply hundreds of times.

Lead-acid storage cells are used in most car batteries. Six two-volt cells connected in a series give the battery an output of twelve volts.

Many other types of cells and batteries are in use today. These range from the tiny mercury cells used in hearing aids to huge fuel cells which have a constant supply of chemical fuel and so never run down.

See also: CAPACITORS, ELECTRICITY, ELECTRIC CURRENT, FUEL CELLS

Battery and Intensive Farming

In intensive farming, animals are kept in just the right conditions of heat and light. This is called battery farming in many countries because the animals or poultry are kept in groups of cages that look like the cells of a battery. They have carefully measured amounts of food that contain all the ingredients needed for healthy growth. This method produces the maximum amount of meat or the largest number of eggs in the shortest possible time.

Intensive farming works very well because it increases the amount of meat, milk or eggs produced by animals or chickens on a certain piece of land. It also cuts down the number of people needed to take care of the animals.

Disease can be a serious problem when many animals are in close contact with each other, so special diets and ways of housing the animals have to be worked out.

Keeping the animals indoors has one big advantage, however: the whole operation does not depend on the weather or the seasons. Meat, egg and milk production can then go on all the year round.

In all intensive farming, the animals producing the eggs or milk and being fattened for meat are kept quite separate from the ones that are going to breed. The breeding stock usually has more room and is carefully chosen to produce as many offspring as possible. Breeding animals are also chosen to put on as much weight as possible from a certain amount of food.

Watching the rate of growth
Animals grow quickly when they are young. As they

Below: Most of our eggs come from battery chickens. The eggs roll out of the front of the cages.

158

near maturity they need more and more food to put on each pound of weight. This is why they are usually killed while they are still quite young.

For example, a broiler chicken (one being reared for its meat) reaches a weight of 4 pounds (2 kilograms) in 7 weeks, when it is usually killed. For each 2¼ pounds (1 kilogram) of feed it eats, it gains 1 pound (0.45 kilogram) in weight. If it is allowed to grow to be an older bird, however, it will soon take 3 pounds (1.4 kilograms) or more of feed to put on each pound of weight.

When animals grow at such a fast rate, their food has to be carefully controlled. They need different kinds of food the older they get. And the rate of growth can also be speeded up by giving them special hormones in their feed.

Broiler chickens

The rearing of broiler chickens is the most efficient kind of intensive farming. Day-old chicks are raised in very large houses, with carefully controlled ventilation, heating and lighting. Feed comes in automatically on a conveyor system and water is piped in. To prevent disease, broilers are usually fed a diet which contains certain medicines.

A modern broiler farm may consist of several chicken houses, each with 15,000 birds in large pens. The birds come from the hatchery as day-old chicks, already vaccinated against some common diseases. From the time the birds come from the hatchery, they may not be handled by people again until they are collected for slaughter.

Because everything is automatic, the entire farm can be run by two or three people. As a result of intensive farming, broiler chickens can be bought cheaply and at any time of the year.

Producing eggs

Most of the eggs we eat come from chickens in battery farms. From three to six pullets (female chickens less than a year old) are placed in each battery cage just as they begin to lay. Feed comes in on a moving conveyor and water is supplied through special pipes from which the chickens can drink. Droppings pass through the wire cage floor onto a moving belt that removes them from the house.

As the eggs are laid, they roll through a gap at the front of the cage. They are collected by hand or by another conveyor.

Light is very important in a battery farm. The amount of light affects the number of eggs a chicken will lay, so the lighting is carefully controlled.

Because of the wire floors, the eggs stay very clean. Chickens producing eggs are not usually given feed with medicines in it. This is because drugs may collect in the eggs. Disease among the birds is kept down

Above: Breeding stock cattle are not usually brought into such close conditions as animals being fattened for their meat. These Holstein cows are eating corn from an automatic feeder.

by keeping them away from all possible infection, especially from their droppings.

Nowadays, chickens lay more and better eggs, and all breeds lay throughout the whole year.

Beef and veal production

Beef cattle are usually fattened in vast feedlots containing many thousand beasts. Feed, which is mainly corn, is supplied from trucks which discharge into feeding troughs as the trucks drive along the feedlot.

The feed is mixed with proteins and vitamins, and the calves can at first gain more than 3 pounds (1.4 kilograms) per day. They are usually killed under 12 months old when they have reached a weight of about 900 pounds (410 kilograms).

In Europe, intensive veal production takes place, especially in Holland and Belgium. Unweaned calves are placed in small pens in darkened houses. They are fed "milk-replacer" and grow very quickly. This makes very soft, white meat.

Other intensive production

Pigs are often raised intensively, and quite a number of different ways have been found to fatten them up quickly and efficiently.

Turkeys are raised in the same way as broiler chickens in large houses. Most of them are killed at an age of about 13 weeks to make small table birds. But when larger turkeys are required, they may be put into barns or yards to finish growing. To keep down fighting, male and female birds are often kept in separate flocks.

See also: FARMING, HORMONES

Bearings

The ancient Egyptians used bearings for moving the huge stones needed for the pyramids. Logs were placed under the stones so that they could be rolled along easily. Many modern bearings work on a similar principle.

Friction

To slide one object over another, a force must be used to overcome the friction between the two surfaces. Friction is the name given to forces that tend to prevent the movement. The friction between rough surfaces is much greater than the friction between smooth surfaces.

When we use a force to overcome friction, some of the energy we use up is changed into heat. For example, when we strike a match, the friction between the match and the box produces enough heat to light the chemicals in the match head. In machines, friction wastes energy and causes moving parts to wear out. Bearings reduce friction and so improve performance.

Bearings can be designed to support moving parts that rotate or slide. Most bearings are used to support rotating parts. The three main types of bearing are rolling element, fluid film and rubbing bearings.

Rolling element bearings

Rolling element bearings use precision-made rollers or balls between a fixed and a moving surface. The most common type of rolling bearing consists of four main parts: an inner ring, or race; a set of rollers or balls; a device called a cage to keep the rolling elements in position; and an outer race. The cage is made of soft steel, brass or plastic resin. All the other parts are made of hard steel so that they can take heavy loads.

In machines where a load presses at right angles to the turning shaft, ball bearings are normally used.

Bearings with rollers can be used to withstand thrust along the shaft. Automobile wheels are often mounted on tapered roller bearings. These are designed to support the weight of the vehicle. They also withstand sideways forces produced when going round corners.

Lubrication

For long life and quiet operation, rolling element bearings must be lubricated with oil or grease. This allows the moving parts to slide over each other easily. Most of these bearings are packed with grease. In heavy industrial machines, where a lot of heat is produced in the bearings, circulating oil is used as the lubricant. Besides making sure the operation of the bearings is smooth, the oil flow also removes the heat. The warmed oil coming from the bearings is cooled before being passed through them again.

Ordinary greases tend to dry up in the VACUUM of outer space. So special greases have been developed for the bearings on vehicles designed to remain in space for long periods.

Fluid film bearings

In fluid film bearings, frictional forces between the sur-

Right: In a rolling bearing, the rollers may be cylindrical, barrel-shaped, tapered or shaped like an hour glass.

Below: A ball journal bearing. The inner race is surrounded by a reinforced cast metal case that houses the ball bearings. The shaft can rotate freely within the outer race. The rolling action greatly reduces friction.

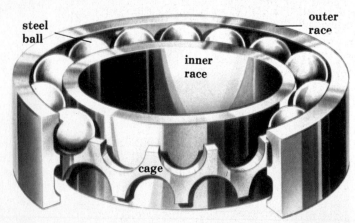

steel ball · outer race · inner race · cage

inner race · steel roller · outer race

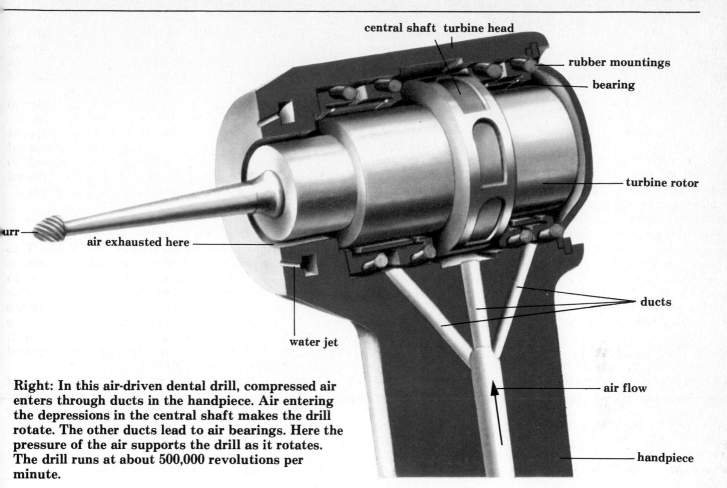

central shaft   turbine head

rubber mountings

bearing

turbine rotor

urr

air exhausted here

ducts

water jet

air flow

handpiece

Right: In this air-driven dental drill, compressed air enters through ducts in the handpiece. Air entering the depressions in the central shaft makes the drill rotate. The other ducts lead to air bearings. Here the pressure of the air supports the drill as it rotates. The drill runs at about 500,000 revolutions per minute.

faces are reduced by a film of fluid, instead of balls or rollers. The fluid is usually oil, but it can be water or even air or other gas. It can be convenient to use water film bearings in a water pump.

The two main kinds of fluid film bearings are the HYDRODYNAMIC and HYDROSTATIC types. In both, the fluid film must force the moving surface away from the fixed one. In the hydrodynamic bearing, the fluid is drawn in by the rotation of the moving part. In the hydrostatic bearing, the fluid is supplied under pressure from an external source.

Hydrodynamic bearings

Most fluid film bearings are hydrodynamic. They are used in machines where the speed of rotation is sufficient to draw in the fluid between the surfaces. Automobile engine crankshaft bearings operate on this principle. Although a pump supplies oil to the bearings, the pressure is not sufficient to separate the surfaces.

As in all hydrodynamic bearings, the surfaces are in contact when starting or stopping, as the speed is too low to draw in the oil. So the bearings have to be made from materials that will permit some rubbing.

Similar bearings using air as a lubricant instead of

liquid are called aerodynamic bearings. These are suitable for high-speed machines with light loads, for example textile spinning equipment.

Hydrostatic bearings

Hydrostatic bearings need a pumped supply of fluid at a pressure high enough to separate the surfaces. Such bearings are used to support heavy loads moving at low speeds. Most hydrostatic bearings resemble hydrodynamic bearings, but with provision for pumping in the fluid.

Aerostatic bearings work on the same principle but use an air film and work at high speed. Dental drills use this type of bearing.

Rubbing bearings

Rubbing bearings made from plastic materials can operate without lubrication, the surfaces making direct contact. Self-lubricating rubbing bearings are made from spongy metal containing oil. Rubbing bearings are cheap to produce, but are suitable only for light duty applications.

See also: AERODYNAMICS, ALLOYS

Bell, electric

The electric bell is used as a doorbell in many houses and apartment buildings. It is a simple and effective way for people to announce their arrival. When a button is pushed on the outside of the building it will set off a ringing noise inside the home.

The electric bell, used as a doorbell in many homes, consists of an ELECTROMAGNET, a pair of electrical contacts, a gong and a striking arm. The arm is mounted by means of a flat spring, so that it can vibrate. At the free end of the arm is a small, rounded weight called a clapper. This is the part that strikes the gong.

How the bell works

The electric bell is operated by means of a battery or power supply unit. Pressing a button on the door connects the supply to the electric bell. The electric current flows through the electromagnet via the pair of contacts. The electromagnet now attracts the arm, causing the clapper to strike the gong.

The movement of the arm also pulls the contacts apart, thus cutting off the supply to the electromagnet. As a result, the electromagnet no longer attracts the arm so it springs back to its original position, allowing the contacts to touch again. The supply to the electromagnet is thus restored, and so the process repeats.

While the pushbutton is held down, the arm will vibrate to and fro, causing continuous ringing. Usually, one of the electrical contacts can be adjusted to change the speed of the vibration.

Different types of bell

Electric buzzers work on the same principle. But there is no gong, and the moving arm is much shorter. Vibrations of the arm are sent through the body of the device to produce the buzzing sound.

Some alarm bells on the outside of stores and offices are operated by electric motors instead of magnets. An arm with a hinged hammer end spins around. The hammer strikes the bell gong several times each second making a continuous noise.

See also: ELECTRIC CURRENT, MAGNETISM

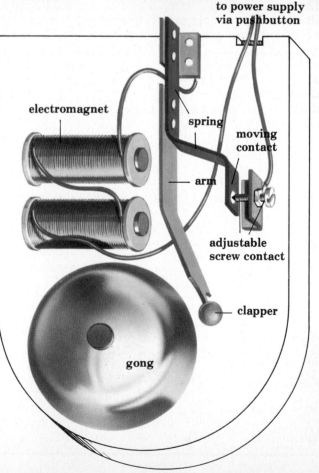

Above right: Testing the coils for electric bells.

Right: A simple electric bell. Current passes through the electromagnet when a pushbutton is pressed. The magnet attracts the arm and the clapper strikes the gong. The contacts separate, so the circuit is broken and the arm springs back. The process repeats.

Bells

Bells seem to be as old as history. Small hand bells have been dug up in what was ancient Assyria—they are more than 3000 years old. And, like most modern bells, they are made of bronze, a tough alloy that gives a good tone and does not rust.

When a bell is struck, the metal it is made of vibrates. This vibration causes movements in the air around the bell and these movements travel through the air to our ears. We hear the bell sound.

The earliest bells had convex sides (widest in the middle, rather like cow bells). From about the 13th century the shape began to change, first to bells with almost straight sides, and then to the bell shape we know today. In China, however, bells stayed drum-shaped.

How a bell is made

Bells are cast in bronze that is about 77 percent copper and 23 percent tin. This is the same kind of bronze that was used for old cannons and Roman swords. The molten metal is poured into a mold that is the exact shape the bell is to be.

The inside part of the mold is called the core. It is built up from bricks covered with clay and smoothed to the shape of the inside of the bell with a molding board. The outside of the mold is called the cope. It is a cast iron case, also lined with clay. Sometimes the clay is mixed with old traditional materials such as goat hair and horse droppings. These burn when the molten metal is poured between the core and the cope and make ventilation holes to help the cooling.

Above: After finishing, the core and outside mold are clamped together, with a space between them. This space is filled with molten metal, as shown in the photograph. The metal takes two days to cool. The outside mold is then lifted off and the clay is cleared off the cast bell.

Left: The way of making a large bell is still done in much the same way as it was in this engraving from the 1850s. The inside core of the mold is built up with clay on a brick foundation. The clay is smoothed out with a molding board. The outside mold is made in a similar way.

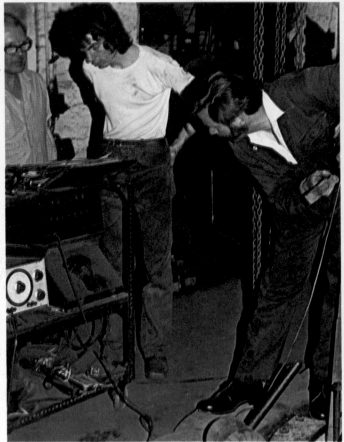

The bell is cast a little thicker than the final bell is to be. (The thicker the metal of a bell, the lower the note it will make when it is struck.) Then the metal inside the bell is carefully shaved away with a lathe until the right pitch sounds.

Ringing bells
Bells in a belfry are hung in a special frame, and there is a freely swinging clapper inside each bell. The traditional way of ringing a bell is by pulling a rope which swings the bell until the open end is almost pointing at the sky. The clapper strikes first one side of the bell, then the other.

Several bells of different pitches are hung together. When they are rung in the right order they play tunes called *peals* or *chimes*. In the United States, chiming is usually carried out by mechanical devices.

About 400 AD, Paulinus, the bishop of Nola in Campania, Italy, is thought to have erected the first bell on a church roof. From this comes our word "campanology," which means the art of bell ringing.

Ship's bell
No one knows for certain when sailors began to use bells on board ship. But by the end of the 17th century

Above left: To make the bell give the desired sound, the inside of the bell is shaved away with a lathe.

Above: The bell is tested with an electronic device which picks up the vibrations through a microphone. The device then compares the vibrations from the bell with a master "tuning fork."

many European vessels had bells on which to strike the hours and half-hours.

The seaman's 24-hour day is divided into watches. Beginning at midnight, each watch is four hours long, with the exception of the period between 4 p.m. and 8 p.m. which is divided into the first and second dog watches—4 to 6 p.m. and 6 to 8 p.m. The ship's bell is struck once for each half-hour that has passed since the beginning of the watch—8.30 is "one bell," 12.00 is "eight bells." Ships' bell strokes are sounded in pairs, with a short interval between each pair.

The folklore of bells
Bells have given rise to many beliefs and superstitions. Bells were rung in ancient Greece to frighten away the avenging spirits when a person died. In the Middle Ages witches were hunted to the sound of a bell, and

evil spirits were frightened away with "bell, book and candle." King Solomon was supposed to have had gold bells on the roof of his temple to keep the birds away.

Bells in the orchestra

In an orchestra, the bells are part of the percussion section. They are tube-shaped bells that can be accurately tuned. Several famous composers have written music which includes the sound of bells. They include Wagner, Berlioz, Puccini, Verdi and Mussorgsky.

See also: BRONZE, MUSICAL INSTRUMENTS, SOUND

Above: A bell is cast to sound at a lower pitch than required so that metal can be removed later to get the required sound. Here is a bell being spun while excess metal is trimmed from inside.

Right: Hand bells are made and tuned in a similar way to large bells. The craftsman in the picture is polishing a bell. A complete set of handbells may have as many as 61 separate bells.

Bicycles

The first bicycle looked very different from the streamlined aluminum models of today. It was invented in France in 1791 and was a strange-looking, two-wheeled wooden vehicle. The front wheel was fixed in position and there were no pedals! Instead the bicycle moved forward when the rider placed his feet on the ground and walked forward.

A serious attempt to improve on this primitive model was made by Baron von Drais de Sauerbrun in 1817. Still without pedals, his bicycle had a wooden frame, large spoked wooden wheels with metal tires, a seat and even an armrest. It could be steered by a bar connected to the front wheel. Bicycling became a popular hobby in Germany, France, America and England, and this early model was known as the "hobby horse."

Early machines

In 1839 the first pedal-operated bicycle was invented by a Scottish blacksmith, Kirkpatrick Macmillan. It is quite likely that he repaired hobby-horses at his forge, but instead of just changing an existing model, he produced a new design with foot pedals driving the rear wheel.

The steerable front wheel was carried on an iron fork fitted to the front of the wooden frame. This was divided at the other end to form a fork for the rear wheel.

The pedals were fitted to the ends of two levers which pivoted on the frame near the front fork. Connecting rods transferred the movement of the levers to cranks (a shaft bent to convert up-and-down movement to circular motion) fitted on the rear axle. Macmillan's machine was the first to prove that a two-wheeled vehicle could be powered by the feet without the rider losing his balance.

Further developments

The opening up of the English and U.S. markets to bicycles meant that by the late 1860s there were many important developments in the design. For example, there were experiments with wheels that had wire spokes, and also the first rubber tires were demonstrated.

Other new changes were the first cycle lamp (a candle in a small box fitted to the handlebars) and a primitive rear brake. This was a spoon or shoe (from where we get the term brake shoes) which was used to slow down the tire by direct contact when the rider pulled a cord fixed to the handlebars.

One of the disadvantages of these bikes was that they traveled only as far as the circumference of one wheel with each complete turn of the pedals. To make them go faster, the front wheel was sometimes as big as 50 inches (130 centimeters) in diameter, while the rear wheel had a diameter of about 24 inches (60 centimeters). Every turn of the pedals turned the big wheel

Draisienne: The rider sat in the seat and "walked" his way around!

Macmillan's machine: The rider moved treadles to turn back wheels.

Penny Farthing: This model was named after the English coins.

once, so the bike traveled further for each turn. This model was nicknamed the Penny Farthing—because of the large (penny) and small (farthing) English coins.

A chain-drive type of bicycle appeared in 1879 with the front wheel driven by cranks. These were found below the center of the wheel and were connected to it by a chain and sprocket (a toothed wheel) arrangement.

By the turn of the century, bicycles were a very popular form of transport. They were cheap and practical, and by 1897 about four million Americans were riding every day.

How a bicycle moves

When the rider pushes the pedals of a bicycle, the pedals turn a sprocket called the chain wheel. A chain, which is fitted over the metal teeth around the edge of

the chain wheel, extends to a smaller sprocket on the rear wheel of the bike and fits over the teeth of this sprocket. The pedals turn the large sprocket which moves the chain. This turns the small sprocket which then turns the rear wheel and the bike moves foward.

Gears

The majority of bikes have gears which are used (as in a car) for when you are traveling faster or slower. They help the rider use the best combination of pedaling effort and pedaling speed. For example, a rider would change into low gear when going uphill. This makes pedaling easier, but the bicycle go slower. On level surfaces, however, the rider would change to a high gear which makes him pedal more slowly, but the bike go faster.

The gears of a multispeed bicycle are sprockets of different sizes. The number of gears controls the range of speeds. For example, if you have a five-speed bike it will have five gears on the rear wheel. If you own a ten-speed bike it will have five gears on the rear wheel and two gears that form the chain wheel.

A mechanism called a "derailleur" changes the chain

> ⭐ ## Did you know?
>
> The world's smallest bicycle was designed and built by Mr Charlie Charles. The bike was ridden in Mr Charles' Las Vegas cabaret act and each wheel measured only 2.12 inches (5.4 centimeters) across.

Far left: The "hobby horse" was very much a toy for the rich. The basic machine shown here has been adapted to carry a lady passenger.

Left: By the late 19th century the "safety" bicycle was the standard design. Charles Terront of France is shown here with the bicycle he raced in 1891.

Cross-frame safety: By 1888, bicycles had wheels the same size.

Roadster: The enclosed chain prevented skirts getting caught.

Ten-speed: The modern bicycle is lighter and more streamlined.

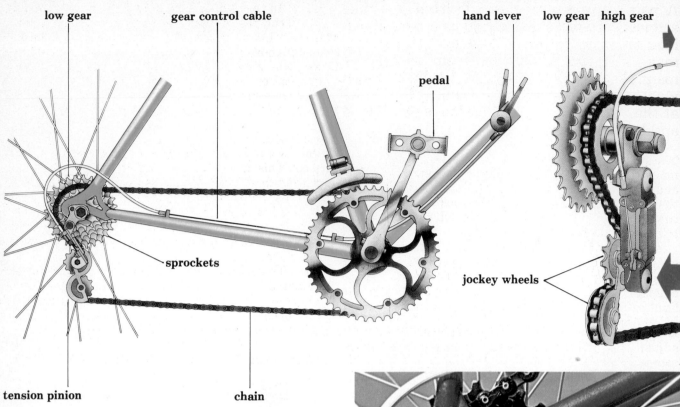

low gear   gear control cable   hand lever   low gear   high gear

pedal

sprockets

jockey wheels

tension pinion   chain

Above: The derailleur gear mechanism. Depression of the small hand lever on the frame increases the tension in the gear control cable. This moves the lever carrying the jockey wheels over the range of sprockets. Each sprocket represents a different gear.

Right: A modern Campagnolo gear mechanism.

from one gear to another. On most bikes with derailleur gears, the rider changes gear by moving two levers on the bike's down tube, but some bikes have gear controls on the handlebars.

Frames

The frame of a bicycle must have two special features for efficient use. It must be rigid and made in one piece so that all the effort from the rider goes into a downward thrust. If, after each push of the pedal, a part of the frame had to move back to its original position before the next push, energy would be wasted.

The frame must also have "give." This is essential because without it all the bumps and roughness in the road would directly affect the rider through the seat and handlebars. This would make a very uncomfortable ride—especially over long distances.

Most frames today are made of high quality steel, but aluminum alloy is used for some lightweight models.

The fastest speed ever achieved on a bicycle was by an American, Allan Abbott, in 1972. He rode in the slipstream of a drag racing car on the Bonneville Salt Flats and went at 138 mph (223 km/h).

See also: MOTORCYCLES

Binoculars

A pair of binoculars is made from two telescopes mounted side by side so a person can look through one with each eye. Binoculars make far away objects seem closer by magnifying them. Also, a three-dimensional view is obtained—this means using both eyes at the same time to give a scene depth, width and height.

The simplest binoculars are opera glasses. These do not make the object very much larger (low magnification) and have a small field of view. This means that most of the scene is cut off, as it is if you look through a long tube. Binoculars of this kind consist of two simple telescopes, each with just two lenses.

A pair of powerful binoculars could also be made from simple telescopes. But these would need to be so long (to give a high magnification) that they would be too clumsy for general use. To overcome this problem, the light path in each side can be folded by means of a glass

Below: A pair of binoculars with a central focus adjustment. The prisms fold the light path to make a compact instrument.

prism. In this way, a long light path and high magnification can be obtained without lengthening the instrument. This arrangement also allows the objective lenses (those closest to the object) to be farther apart than the viewer's eyes. A greater effect of depth is obtained in this way. Another advantage is that there is room for much larger front lenses. Larger lenses let in more light and, therefore, form a brighter image.

Binocular construction

Binoculars are usually focused by turning a central wheel. This causes the two telescope tubes to slide in or out together. To compensate for differences between a person's eyes, one of the eyepiece lenses can be adjusted separately at the start. The two parts of the binoculars are hinged together. This allows the user to adjust the separation to suit the distance between his or her eyes.

The lenses are usually made from two types of glass cemented together. This construction is used to cancel out color distortion. In prismatic binoculars, the telescopes form images that are upside down. But the prisms turn the images up the right way again.

See also: CAMERA, PRISM, TELESCOPE

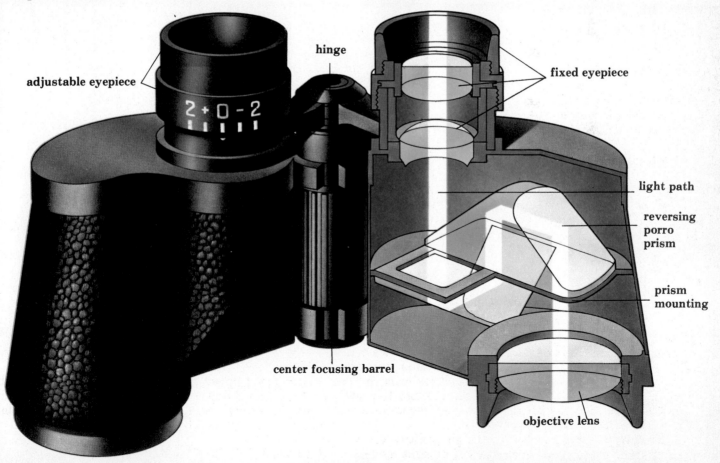

adjustable eyepiece — hinge — fixed eyepiece — light path — reversing porro prism — prism mounting — center focusing barrel — objective lens

2 + 0 - 2

Biology

Biology is the study of living things, or organisms. Organisms can be divided into two main groups—plants and animals. So biology can be divided into two main branches. Botany is the study of plants, and zoology is the study of animals.

In biology, as in any science, it is important to understand what is meant by the various terms that we use to avoid confusion. Even when we are talking about plants and animals, can we be sure that other people mean the same as we do by these words? And do we all mean the same when we describe something as living? Many people do not think about questions like this for the answers seem obvious. But it is often the simplest questions that are the most important and the most difficult to answer.

What is life?
We say that animals, such as cats and dogs, are alive as they can move about, eat and drink, breathe, grow, reproduce, rest and play. Plants are obviously alive if they grow and produce flowers and seeds. Many objects around us seem to show none of these signs, so we regard them as lifeless, or non-living.

To define life, we might say that living things can reproduce themselves. But this definition is not accurate because some kinds of plants and animals are unable to reproduce. The mule, for example, results only from a male ass (donkey) mating with a female horse. Mules cannot reproduce themselves, yet they are clearly living creatures.

Growth and movement
Growth is another characteristic of organisms. But it cannot be used to tell the difference between living and non-living things. For the flame from a match can soon grow into a blaze if it is "fed" with paper or other material that burns. And a crystal can be made to grow if it is hung in a solution of the substance from which it is made. This is a project you will find in Volume 25.

Any kind of life has a recognizable structure, but this, again, is a property of crystals. So it does not necessarily indicate the presence of life. Movement is another property of living things. Most animals move about to find their food, and plants move slowly when growing, or opening and closing their flowers. But movement does not always accompany life.

If you want to grow some flowers, you buy a packet of seeds to plant. The seeds are absolutely still and show no signs of life. Yet they are living organisms. Planting them enables the next stage in the life cycle to begin. They undergo remarkable changes and start to develop into mature plants.

Of course, in a garden or zoo, we can all recognize many types of plants and animals. But problems arise because many organisms are quite different from what we usually think of as plants and animals. For example, the fine, white powdery "bloom" found on grape skins is actually a form of plant life.

Appearances can, therefore, be deceptive. So biologists have to bear in mind all the properties of known living things when trying to decide whether or not something is a form of life. For there is no simple definition that applies to all of the millions of forms that have evolved since life began.

Branches of biology
At one time, biologists studied either plants or animals. But the invention of the microscope revealed that most plants and animals have something in common. They are made up of tiny units called cells. The microscope also revealed a whole new world of simple, single-celled plants and animals. These and other discoveries changed the way in which biology was studied.

The numerous branches of biology now include: bacteriology, which concerns only the tiny organisms called bacteria; biochemistry, the study of chemical changes in living things; biophysics, the use of physics to study life; anatomy, the study of the structure of living things; and ecology, which is the study of relationships between living things and their environment (surroundings).

See also: BACTERIA, CELLS, MICROSCOPE

Below: An amoeba seen under a very strong microscope. This is one of a group of tiny, single-celled organisms that form the lowest division of the animal kingdom. Although the amoeba is a simple life form, it has gone through many changes in the course of evolutionary history.

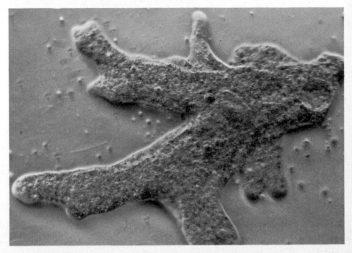

Biorhythms

Many people who have to get up at a certain time every morning wake up just before the alarm goes off. There seems to be some mysterious clock in their brain which wakes them up at just the right time. This is a "biological clock" and it is worked by biorhythms.

Our lives are constantly affected by everything around us. The earth rotates on its axis once every day, giving us light and darkness. The seasons change as the earth goes around the sun. We are surrounded by changes in light, temperature, gravity, air pressure and many other things that we hardly notice.

Along with all plants and animals, people have become used to a 24-hour cycle. Scientists call this the CIRCADIAN RHYTHM. We are only really aware of the most obvious circadian rhythm—sleeping and being awake. But many other things vary at certain times during the day and night. Our body temperature, pulse rate, blood pressure, rate of breathing and many other life processes vary regularly in time with our invisible biological clocks. In fact, we can only stay in good health if all these body rhythms work together.

Morning and afternoon people
The rhythms vary from person to person. Some people like to get up early and do their best work in the morning; others have difficulty waking up and work best later in the day. This seems to have something to do with body temperature. Each day a person's temperature rises and falls quite regularly by two or three degrees. These temperature changes always happen at the same time of day. The highest temperatures usually happen in the afternoon or evening for a person who sleeps at night. It has been found that this period of high temperature is usually the person's favorite time of day.

The lowest temperature happens during sleep, and it rises as we get close to the time when we have to get up. People who are bright and active when they first get up usually have a temperature rise that happens earlier than normal. Those who awaken slowly and have difficulty getting up have a temperature cycle that is just beginning to rise at the time when they get up.

Right: Plants have their biological clocks, too. This can be seen quite easily from this flower which folds its petals at night (top) and opens them during the day (bottom). If the flower is taken into the laboratory and kept in the same light, night and day, it goes on closing its petals when it thinks it should be night. However, after a while its clock goes wrong. It no longer works to a 24-hour schedule, and eventually the rhythm of opening and closing the petals fades away.

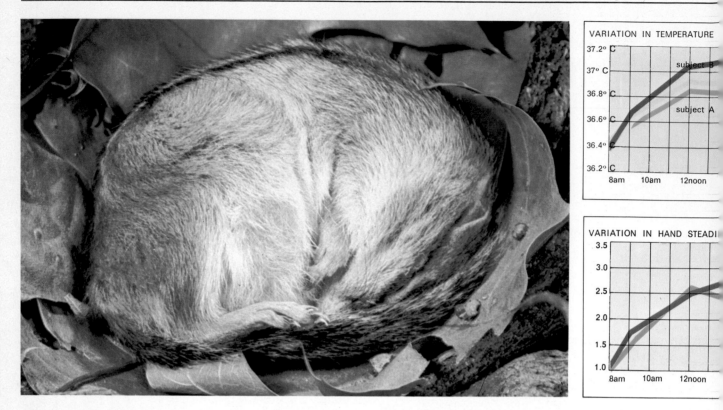

VARIATION IN TEMPERATURE

subject B

subject A

37.2° C
37° C
36.8° C
36.6° C
36.4° C
36.2° C

8am   10am   12noon

VARIATION IN HAND STEADI

3.5
3.0
2.5
2.0
1.5
1.0

8am   10am   12noon

Above: A chipmunk passes the winter in the deep sleep of hibernation. This is one of the regular events in the lives of animals that are controlled by a biological clock.

Our pulse rate also seems to follow our body temperature. It also rises to its highest rate during the afternoon and slows up during the night.

There are other things which change regularly during the circadian 24-hour rhythm. Certain GLANDS work harder at certain times of the day. When the glands work harder, we feel more active. When the glands slow up, we feel tired and lazy.

Even the rate at which our kidneys make urine varies throughout the day. When we are asleep they make very little, so we seldom have to go to the bathroom during the night.

The senses change
Our senses of hearing, taste and smell have rhythms, too. These senses are usually at their best between 5 p.m. and 7 p.m. This is the time of day when most people enjoy eating and listening to music.

The body's rhythms are very constant
To see whether body rhythms can be made to change, people have lived for up to six months in deep caves with no sunlight. In these conditions of constant light and temperature, the body still keeps to its 24-hour

Above right: People vary in the pattern of their daily rhythms. In the chart at the top, Subject A's body temperature was highest at noon. Subject B's body temperature was highest at 6 p.m. (To draw these graphs, the subjects' temperatures were taken every hour over a period of 20 days, and averaged out.) The bottom chart shows what happened when the same two people were tested to see how steady their hands were throughout the day. Every hour they were asked to place a sharp-pointed needle in a tiny hole. If the needle touched the sides of the hole, they failed the test. The scale on the left of the chart shows their success rate. It can be seen that Subject A did best at noon and Subject B at 6 p.m., exactly the same times as their highest body temperatures. A is a "morning person," B is an "evening person."

rhythms. But after a while, with nothing to check the body's clock, the average person's systems tend to start working to a 25-hour day.

Some things do upset the body's rhythms for a while. If a person changes from day to night work or goes on a long jet flight, his internal clock becomes confused. If someone flies from Los Angeles to London, his or her body will be working 11 hours out of step. If the person has a meeting at 11 a.m. London time his internal clock will be acting as though it is midnight. He should be going to bed, with hours of sleep ahead of him.

Scientists believe that the body adjusts to this "jet

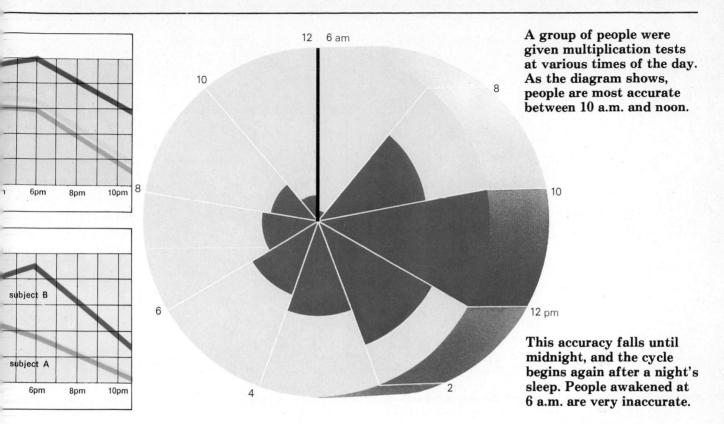

A group of people were given multiplication tests at various times of the day. As the diagram shows, people are most accurate between 10 a.m. and noon.

This accuracy falls until midnight, and the cycle begins again after a night's sleep. People awakened at 6 a.m. are very inaccurate.

lag" at a rate of about one hour a day. It would therefore take a person about 11 days to adjust after a flight from Los Angeles to London. Studies of airline pilots and flight attendants who travel a lot across many time zones have shown that some of their body functions can become very irregular.

Other body rhythms

The daily 24-hour body rhythm is only one of the rhythms of life. There are also monthly, seasonal and yearly cycles. The most obvious of these is the female MENSTRUAL CYCLE. This affects a woman's physical and emotional state at monthly intervals. These effects can, in some women, include changes in breathing rate, sight and likelihood of catching infections.

Men can also have monthly rhythms in which their moods change in a regular cycle.

Diseases which often occur periodically are well-known to doctors. Common diseases of this kind include epilepsy, migraine and some kinds of fevers and swellings. It is also known that a gland called the thyroid gland makes a "summer hormone" which helps to reduce body heat. Somehow the gland gives out this hormone just before the hot summer months.

Animals and plants

Animals and plants use their body clocks in many ways. It is important to a bat in a dark cave or a scorpion down its hole to know that the sun has set and that

it is time to wake up and go outside to find food.

Bees use their internal clocks when they go to find food, too. They tend to visit the same flowers at exactly the same time, day after day. It has also been found that some flowers produce most of their nectar at a particular time of the day.

Normally, biological clocks do not have to be completely accurate. But a very accurate time sense is needed by birds and animals that MIGRATE. It seems that animals may NAVIGATE by "sightings" of the sun and stars. But the position of the sun and stars is never fixed in the sky. The animal needs to know the exact time difference between one position and another so that it can keep on a certain course.

Did you know?

As doctors begin to understand our body rhythms, they are using them to help their patients. They now know that there is a best time of the day to give someone a particular drug, and sometimes it is better to perform a surgical operation early or late in the day.

lots of sunspots on the sun. When there are a lot of sunspots there are many huge flares on the sun. These flares are so big they change the earth's magnetism and can sometimes move a compass needle. It has been shown that our brains are sensitive to magnetic changes.

Did you know?

Experiments have been carried out with people who are put into a hypnotic sleep. It was found that their biological clock would wake them up at a certain time to carry out a particular task, even while under hypnosis.

It is only since the early 1960s that scientists have been trying to find out about biorhythms in people. It now seems likely that what they are discovering about these mysterious internal clocks will play a much bigger part in the future in how doctors look at and treat the human body.

See also: ASTRONOMY, BRAIN, MAGNETISM

Above: Miners coming out of a coal mine after a night shift. After a few days of night shift their biorhythms settle down. They relax in the morning and sleep in the afternoon. But too many changes from day to night shift can cause them stress.

Right: Sometimes two different biorhythms are combined. Limpets feed every 12½ hours whenever their part of the shore is covered by the tide. They also feed at night, even at low tide, when the rocks are not dried out by the sun.

We need to know more
Several reasons have been suggested as to how our body rhythms start. Babies don't appear to have any rhythms during the first few weeks of life. They sleep and wake up at any time of day or night. It seems that they have to learn to do things by a 24-hour clock.

Some scientists believe that people can be affected by changes in electrical fields, RADIATIONS from space and magnetism. A study of mental patients seems to show that some of them become more excited when there are

Blast Furnace

For hundreds of years, the blast furnace has provided the main means of iron production. In the furnace, iron ore is heated by burning coke (a byproduct of coal) in a blast of air. The heat causes chemical reactions to take place, and the iron ore is converted into iron.

Early furnaces
The blast furnaces that were in use in the Middle Ages used bellows to provide the necessary blast of hot air needed in iron production. Major improvements in the process were made in the 1700s and 1800s. In 1709, Abraham Darby became the first person to use coke as a heat source instead of charcoal. And, in 1766, John Wilkinson introduced the use of steam power to force the air into the furnace.

The technique of preheating the air used in the blast was developed in 1828 by James Neilson. In 1831, the Germans found that some of the carbon monoxide formed in the furnace could be drawn off and used to help heat the air blast.

Structure and siting
Modern blast furnaces are large, tower-like buildings, often more than 100 feet (30 meters) high. Above the furnace, another 100 feet or so is taken up by gas pipes and equipment for loading the furnace. The hearth of the furnace measures up to about 45 feet (14 meters).

Below: The charge enters at the top and falls past the open bell valve. The bell is then closed. The charge passes the lower bell and falls into the furnace. As only one bell is open at a time, the hot gas escapes from the furnace.

Blast furnaces used to be built close to supplies of iron ore and coal suitable for making into coke. But now the raw materials often have to be brought in from other countries. The furnaces are mostly sited near ports or major waterways which avoids the high cost of having to transport the raw materials over land. The overall cost of producing the iron is greatly reduced.

The chemical process
The type of chemical reaction that converts iron ore into iron is called REDUCTION. Iron ore consists mainly of iron oxide, a combination of iron and oxygen. The reduction process removes the oxygen from the ore, so that iron is formed.

In the modern blast, coke is burned in hot air. Coke

Below: Cross section of a modern blast furnace. The charge of coke, iron ore and limestone is taken to the top of the furnace in skips. The iron and slag formed are removed from the bottom.

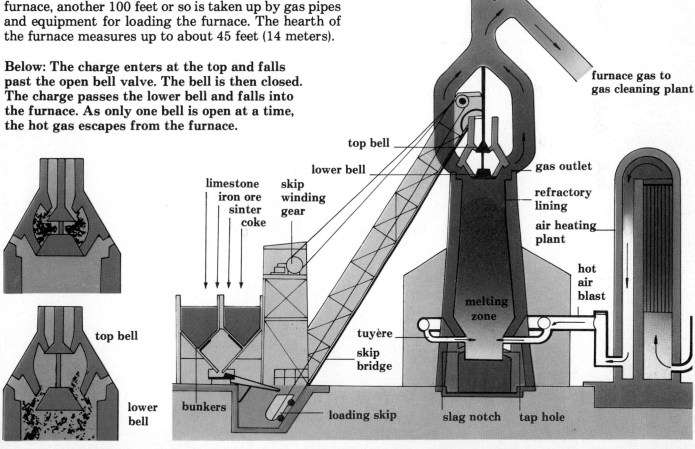

Above left: The pipe coming from near the top of this blast furnace removes waste gases.

Above right: A stream of molten iron being tapped from the bottom of the blast furnace.

consists mainly of carbon. This combines with oxygen from the air to form the gas carbon monoxide. The reaction is represented by the following equation:

$$2C \ + \ O_2 \ = \ 2CO$$
carbon   oxygen   carbon monoxide

The carbon monoxide then combines with the oxygen in the iron ore to form carbon dioxide gas. In this reaction, the iron ore is reduced to iron. The equation representing this chemical reaction is as follows:

$$Fe_2O_3 \ + \ 3CO \ = \ 2Fe \ + \ 3CO_2$$
iron ore   carbon monoxide   iron   carbon dioxide

These equations describe the main reactions that take place in the blast furnace. However, the process is actually more complicated. For iron ore contains other iron compounds. And both carbon from the coke and carbon monoxide play a part in the reduction process. Also, the iron produced is not pure. It contains about 4 percent of carbon. In fact, without this carbon content, the blast furnace process would not work. For pure iron melts at 2300 degrees F (1530 degrees C), which is too

high a temperature for practical commercial operation. However, the presence of carbon in the iron reduces the melting point to about 2100 degrees F (1150 degrees C). As the furnace operates above this temperature, the iron is produced in liquid form, so it can be collected and run off (tapped) as a liquid.

Furnace operation

The solid material, or burden, fed into the top of the blast furnace consists of iron ore, coke and limestone. The limestone helps to absorb impurities in the ore, such as clay and sand.

Air is preheated to about 1800 degrees F (1000 degrees C) and blown through vents near the bottom of the furnace. As the hot air passes up the furnace, it ignites the coke and thus starts the first part of the chemical process. Carbon monoxide is formed, and this reduces the iron ore to iron. The burning coke raises the temperature in the furnace, so that the iron produced is liquid. It collects at the bottom of the furnace.

Impurities in the ore combine with the limestone to form a waste material called slag. This floats on the molten iron. The slag and iron are drawn off separately in their molten state.

Other methods of making iron are in use. But the blast furnace process seems likely to remain the main method of large-scale iron production.

See also: IRON AND STEEL

Blood

Blood is vital to every cell in our bodies. It carries food and oxygen to all the cells and collects their waste. It also acts as the body's police force, arresting any foreign invaders such as unwanted bacteria and other germs.

The average man has about 10 pints (5.7 liters) of blood in his body. Women have slightly less and a child weighing 100 pounds (45 kilograms) may have only 6 pints (3.4 liters). People living in high altitudes have more blood than people who live at sea level. Their bodies need more blood because there is less oxygen the higher one goes and more blood is needed to capture enough of the necessary oxygen.

Parts of the blood

Around 45 percent of the blood is made up of tiny cells, each designed for a special task. Of these cells the most important are the red cells (red corpuscles) and the white cells (white corpuscles). They float in a pale yellow liquid called plasma, made up mostly of water. The red and white cells are so small that just one drop of blood will contain as many as 25 million red cells and 400,000 white ones.

Many parts of the body are constantly hard at work to keep the blood flowing round the body through a network of blood vessels. The heart is a pump that pushes the blood around. Blood flows from the heart through arteries and returns to the heart through veins. The lungs put oxygen into the blood. The kidneys keep the blood free from poisons, and the liver and the intestines supply the blood with food.

Right: Blood travels around the body through a vast network of blood vessels. The heart pumps blood rich in oxygen and food into the arteries (red). The arteries carry the blood to all parts of the body. The blood returns to the heart through the veins (blue).

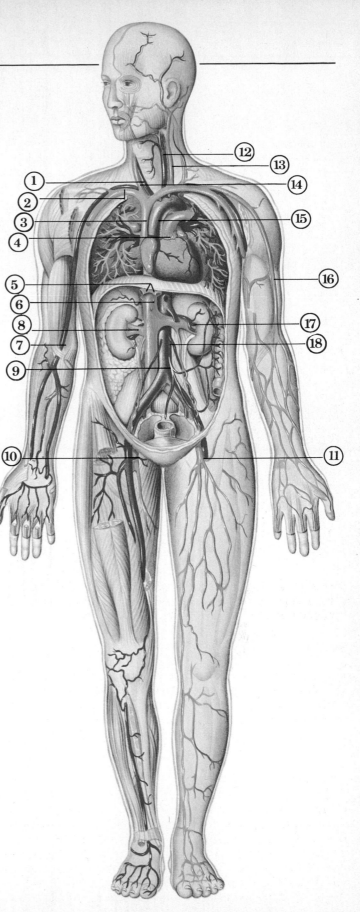

MAIN BLOOD VESSELS

1 Artery to brain
2 Artery to neck and arms
3 Superior vena cava from head, neck and arms
4 Vein from lungs
5 Veins from liver
6 Inferior vena cava from lower body
7 Artery to upper limbs
8 Vein from kidney
9 Large artery
10 Artery to hips, thighs and knees
11 Great vein from lower limbs
12 Artery to neck, face and scalp
13 Jugular vein from brain
14 Vein from brain
15 Aortic arch from heart
16 Vein from lower arm
17 Artery to kidney
18 Artery to small intestine

Right: The diagram shows how blood flows around the body. Bright red blood, rich in oxygen, is pumped by the heart into the arteries. These branch out and get smaller as they carry oxygen to all parts of the body. As tiny capillaries, they link up with equally tiny veins. The veins carry dark red blood (shown blue) away from the tissues. The dark blood contains waste carbon dioxide. The veins come together to form larger veins. These eventually take blood back to the heart. The heart pumps the dark blood to the lungs, where it gives up its waste carbon dioxide and takes in more oxygen. The bright red blood returns to the heart, to be pumped around the body again.

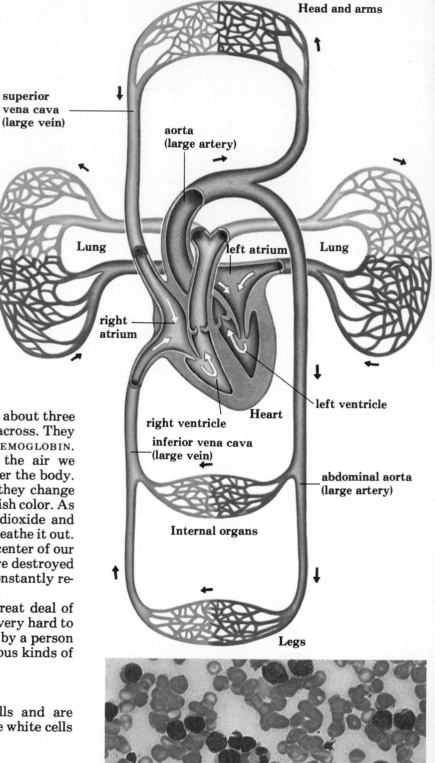

The red blood cells

The red blood cells are tiny round cushions about three thousandths of an inch (0.008 centimeter) across. They get their red color from a substance called HEMOGLOBIN. The hemoglobin picks up oxygen from the air we breathe into our lungs and carries it all over the body. When the red cells give up their oxygen, they change from being bright red to a dark red or purplish color. As they change, they pick up waste carbon dioxide and carry it back to the lungs, from where we breathe it out.

Red cells are made in the marrow at the center of our bones. About five million red blood cells are destroyed in our bodies every second, but they are constantly replaced by new ones.

When a person gives blood or loses a great deal of blood, his or her bone marrow has to work very hard to replace it. There are many diseases caused by a person not having enough red cells. They are various kinds of anemia.

The white blood cells

The white blood cells look like tiny balls and are slightly bigger than the red blood cells. The white cells are the body's disease fighting force.

Right: Human blood as seen through a powerful microscope. The dark purple patches are white cells that have been stained. The red blood cells look pink.

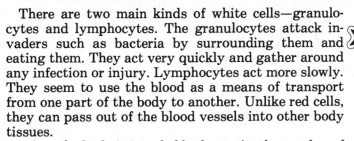

Left: The blood sample on the left is from an artery. It is bright red and full of oxygen when it has just left the lungs. The dark red sample on the right has given up its oxygen and is carrying waste carbon dioxide back to the lungs. There it will collect more oxygen.

There are two main kinds of white cells—granulocytes and lymphocytes. The granulocytes attack invaders such as bacteria by surrounding them and eating them. They act very quickly and gather around any infection or injury. Lymphocytes act more slowly. They seem to use the blood as a means of transport from one part of the body to another. Unlike red cells, they can pass out of the blood vessels into other body tissues.

When the body is invaded by bacteria, the number of white blood cells goes up three or four times. If a cut is infected by bacteria, white cells rush to the wound and surround the bacteria. The pus that forms at the cut is a mixture of dead white cells and the bacteria they have surrounded. White cells will even attack and break down such large invaders as wood splinters and thorns. And it is the white cells that carry away clotted blood and dead tissue after wounds have healed.

How and why our blood clots

Although we can lose up to one-seventh of our blood without any ill-effects, a greater loss can be very serious. Most parts of the body can work for a time with less blood, but the brain cannot. It must have a constant supply.

So our bodies have a system that prevents the blood escaping. This is called clotting—the hardening of blood around a wound. Clotting is the work of special blood cells called platelets. These cells are much smaller than red cells. There are about 15 million of them in

Did you know?

If all the blood vessels in our body could be laid end to end they would total about 100,000 miles (160,000 kilometers) in length. This is long enough to stretch four times around the earth.

every drop of blood. When a blood vessel is damaged, platelets gather around and stick to the injured place and to each other. They form a kind of plug. As they stick together they send out substances that help the blood to clot.

The best-known clotting disease is hemophilia. This is an inherited disease that affects only males, although women pass it on to their sons. It is caused by the absence of one of the substances that make the blood clot. The slightest cut can lead to bleeding that cannot be stopped. Hemophilia affected the family of the Czars of Russia. It is quite a rare disease, affecting about one boy in 10,000.

See also: BLOOD TYPING, BRAIN, CELLS, DIGESTIVE SYSTEM, HEART

Blood Typing

There are several different groups of human blood. Blood from some groups cannot safely be given to people with different blood groups. This is why doctors must find out which blood group a patient has before he or she can be given a blood transfusion.

Most people's blood is one of the four main groups, A, B, AB or O. People of types A or B can receive blood from people of type O, and they can give blood to people of type AB, but they cannot exchange with each other.

People who are in the AB group can give blood only to other ABs, but they can receive blood from any group.

People with type O blood can give to people of all other groups, but can only receive blood from other Os. In practice, however, it is safest only to give people blood of exactly the same group.

If the wrong blood is given to a person, the patient's blood plasma will attack the donor's red blood cells and destroy them. This is very dangerous.

The Rhesus factor

Doctors carrying out experiments with Rhesus monkeys discovered another important fact about our blood. A person either has Rhesus-positive (Rh-positive) blood—he or she has the Rhesus factor—or Rh-negative blood—he or she does not have the Rhesus factor.

When an Rh-negative person is given blood from an Rh-positive person, the Rh-negative's blood develops ANTIBODIES to fight the foreign invaders. If another Rh-positive blood transfusion is given, the patient may become very ill.

We inherit our blood type from our parents. This can cause problems with certain Rh types. If an Rh-positive man marries an Rh-negative woman, she may have an Rh-positive baby. This may cause the woman to develop an anti-Rh substance in her blood. If she should have a second Rh-positive baby, this anti-Rh substance may fight against the baby's red cells and make it very ill. Today, the mother can be treated against this happening. She is given a vaccine that works against Rh disease.

See also: **BLOOD, CELLS, HEART**

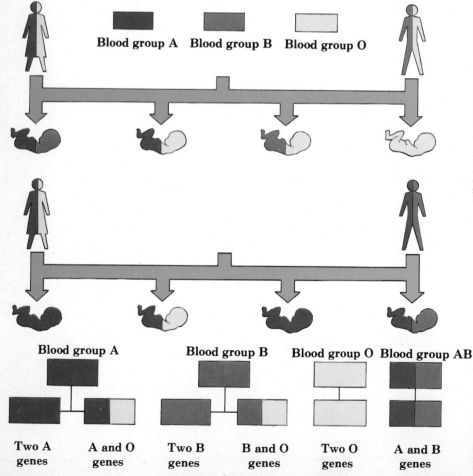

Blood group A   Blood group B   Blood group O

Left: We inherit our blood types from our parents. The diagram show how this works. If a woman with group A and O genes marries a man with B and O genes, they can have babies with AB genes, AO genes, BO genes and O genes. But if the same woman married a man with AB genes, they could not have an O baby. An O baby must inherit an O gene from each parent. These parents can have an A baby, an AO baby or an AB baby.

Blood group A   Blood group B   Blood group O   Blood group AB

| Two A genes | A and O genes | Two B genes | B and O genes | Two O genes | A and B genes |

Blood tests are often used to find out whether a man is a child's father. These tests can show that the child is not related to the man, as the diagram shows. But the tests cannot prove that a man is a baby's father.

Boat Building

As long ago as 2000 BC the Egyptians were building boats from wood. Today, light craft are still made from wood but many boats are now built from a glass-reinforced plastic (GRP). With this method, boats can be built with no joints where water might get in.

Simple boats, such as the dugout canoe, can be carved out of logs. But building boats from lengths (planks) of wood wastes less wood. It also means boats can be made from the narrowest tree trunks.

Plank construction is a highly skilled craft in which numerous wooden pieces are used to build a strong, stable and watertight hull. The two main styles of plank construction are called clinker and carvel.

Clinker construction
In a clinker-built boat, the shape of the hull is formed by bending and fixing planks around one or more mold pieces. The main feature of this type of construction is that the planks overlap. After the planking has been completed, light wooden frames are steamed or sawed to shape. The frames are then fixed to the interior of the hull to strap the planking together. This makes sure that the boat will not fall apart if one of the planks splits along the grain of the wood.

Boats made from clinker construction are very light, but the overlapping edges (lands) of the planks do tend to wear, and it is difficult to keep the planking watertight once it has been disturbed. Clinker construction is, therefore, normally used only for small, light craft, such as rowboats.

Carvel construction
In carvel construction, wooden planks are fitted edge to edge over a completed framework. This determines the shape of the hull and also supports the structure. The framework consists of a piece called the keel, which

Left: A carvel-built boat. Note how the edges of the planks fit smoothly together.

Below: A clinker-built boat. The overlapping planks are fitted from the bottom up.

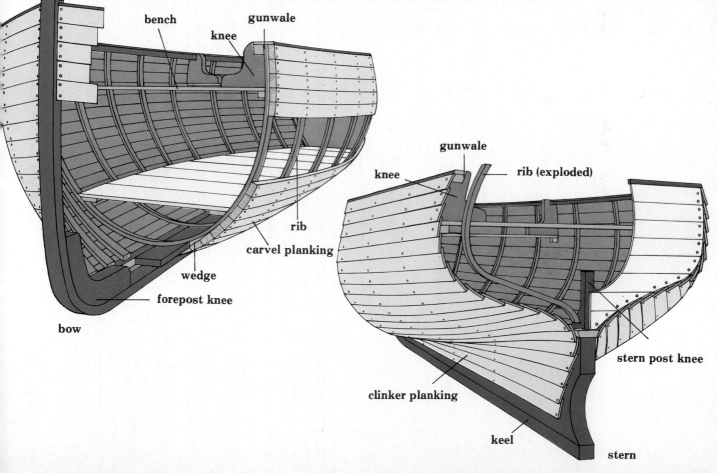

bench · gunwale · knee · rib · carvel planking · wedge · forepost knee · bow

gunwale · knee · rib (exploded) · stern post knee · clinker planking · keel · stern

runs along the center of the boat. The framing across the boat is usually sawed timber. This is cut from suitable branches so that grain lies roughly in the required curves. By avoiding cutting across the grain, a strong frame is obtained. The frames are strapped together inside with full-length planks called stringers. To make the boat watertight, a sealing material called calking compound is hammered between the outside planks.

Plywood boats

Boat building techniques using plywood were developed in the 1920s, mostly in the United States. Plywood is made by gluing thin sheets of wood together. The grain in adjacent sheets is at right angles. This gives the plywood strength and resistance against splitting. The invention of waterproof resin adhesives made it possible to make water-resistant "marine grade" plywood for boats. Plywood quickly became popular for building bulkheads—the upright wall divisions of the hull. Later, plywood became commonly used for the planking skins of cheap small craft.

At first, flat sheets of plywood were bent into shape, but often the plywood could not be bent into exactly the right shape. To overcome this problem, a new technique was developed. The plywood was made over a curved mold of the hull. This type of building, called molded plywood construction, is now used for high-quality racing yachts. The technique is expensive, but gives great strength and light weight.

To build the hull, extremely thin layers of wood are glued over the mold until the required thickness is obtained. If a cold-setting adhesive is used, each layer of wood is held down with staples until the glue sets. In hot molded construction, each layer is held in place by air bags or a vacuum press.

The mold is then moved into an oven so that the hot-setting glue quickly hardens. After removing the mold from the oven, the next layer of wood is applied. Sometimes the keel, ribs and other parts of the boat are of molded construction, too.

Below: The bottom hull section of a molded plywood racing yacht. It has already been heated in the large, cylindrical oven at the rear to set the glue in the plywood. Here the hull section is being lifted from its mold.

Above: Fixing aluminum plates onto the aluminum hull frame of a racing yacht.

Above right: Making a hull by spreading concrete on a mesh-covered frame.

Glass-reinforced plastic

Today, most boats are made from a kind of plastic called polyester resin. This is reinforced with glass fiber to form glass-reinforced plastic (GRP). The finely spun glass fiber is either cut into suitable lengths or woven to make a cloth.

Usually, a hollow mold of the hull is first coated with wax or another material to prevent resin sticking to it. A layer of resin is then applied by spraying or by brush. A supporting layer of glass fiber is placed on the resin and pressed down with a roller. Further layers of resin and glass fiber are applied until the hull is just the right thickness. After a short period of hardening, the hull can be removed from the mold. Then, over a period of several weeks, the hull gradually reaches full hardness.

Sometimes, a mixture of resin and chopped glass fibers is applied to the mold using a hand-held spray gun. As before, the coating is rolled down firmly onto the mold. Another technique is to soak mats of glass fiber in resin and then apply them to the mold. To improve stiffness and reduce weight, a sandwich con-struction can be used. Balsa wood or foam plastic is placed between layers of GRP.

The normal building process starts with the construc-tion of a solid, full-size plastic model of the hull. This model is called the PLUG. A hollow mold is then formed on the plug, using the same process as for hull construc-tion. The plug is expensive to make, but many molds can be formed on it and used for the mass production of the boat. When hard, the hulls are ground and sanded until smooth, and then painted.

The main advantage of GRP construction is that the hull has no joints where water might enter. The hull is also easier to look after than one made from wood.

Other materials

Besides wood and GRP, many other materials are used to make boat hulls. These materials include cast foam plastic, plastic sheet, steel, aluminum alloys and con-crete. Welded steel hulls are popular for larger craft.

High-performance yachts and small, light craft often have hulls made of an aluminum alloy. Special alloys have been produced to resist wear in salt water.

A cheap, but strong hull can be made by covering a metal frame with concrete. This kind of construction is now popular in developing countries.

See also: SHIP BUILDING

Bombs

A bomb is a hollow case that holds explosive or destructive chemicals. Bombs may be dropped from the air, thrown or placed in position and will explode when they hit the target, or through a special timing device. The term bomb comes from the Latin word "bombus," meaning a deep hollow sound.

Development of bombing

Shortly after balloons were invented in 1783, attempts were made to drop bombs by air. In 1849, in the Austro-Venetian war, the Austrians loaded paper hot-air balloons with small bombs. Time fuses were fitted to the bombs, and the balloons were dropped so that they drifted toward Venice. These first flying bombs frightened the Venetians, but caused little damage.

Strangely, this technique was used again in 1944. The Japanese released about 1000 hydrogen-filled

Right: Some of the bombs used in World War II.

Below: A short-barreled cannon used in the 14th century and called a bombard. Because the shot that was fired from these weapons was projected upward and fell onto the enemy, the word bomb is still used to describe ammunition that is dropped on the enemy.

paper balloons carrying bombs toward the United States and Canada. However, most of these fell in remote areas, and the technique was a failure.

Successful bombing from the air became possible early this century with the development of the airplane. In 1911, the Italians were the first to drop bombs from an airplane. They dropped four 4.5-pound (2-kilogram) converted hand grenades on a Turkish camp in Libya. This caused more annoyance than damage; the Turks complained about unfair methods! However, bombing tactics improved steadily, and it soon became possible to deliver heavy bombs to distant targets.

During World War I, both airships and airplanes were used for bombing raids. German Zeppelin airships made more than 200 flights over London, dropping some 200 tons of bombs and causing enormous damage.

Bombing played a much greater role in World War II. During this time, the Allies dropped about two million tons of bombs on Germany and German-occupied territories. Since then, air bombardment has played a large part in other international conflicts.

In the early 1970s, laser equipment was developed for use in bombers. The apparatus sends out a beam that guides the bombs to their targets with pinpoint accuracy.

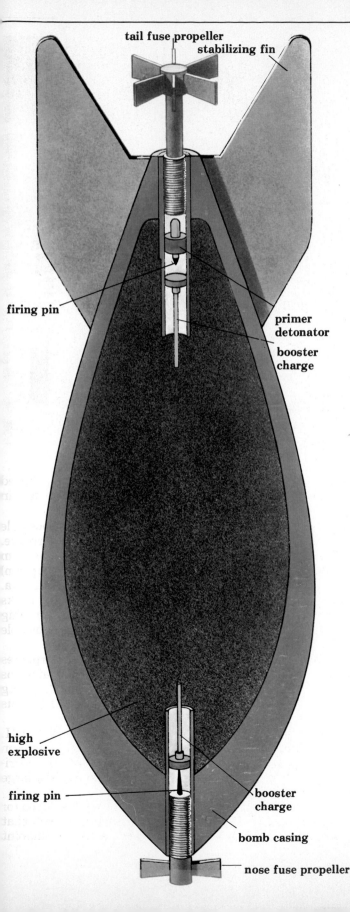

tail fuse propeller
stabilizing fin
firing pin
primer detonator
booster charge
high explosive
firing pin
booster charge
bomb casing
nose fuse propeller

Above: A Halifax bomber of the British Royal Air Force being loaded with bombs in 1941. During World War II, the Allied air forces dropped two million tons of bombs in Europe, and a similar amount in Japan and the Far East.

Left: A general-purpose bomb fitted with two fuses. The air turns the propellers until the firing pins contact the booster charges.

Bomb design

The early bombs dropped from aircraft were ordinary shells with fins and fuses added. Because the bombs were thrown by hand, they were generally quite small, and accuracy was poor. Today's heavy aerial bombs are dropped by releasing them from a rack on the underside of the aircraft.

Most bombs dropped from aircraft have four main parts: a body packed with explosive; a fin assembly to stabilize the bomb in flight; one or more fuses; and a device to arm the bomb at the moment of release. Arming a bomb is like releasing the safety catch on a gun. It prepares the bomb for detonation (setting off). The body (casing) of the bomb usually has a smooth, streamlined shape and a pointed nose. A simple tail fin assembly ensures a smooth flight. A parachute is sometimes used to steady the bomb on its way to the target.

The design of the bomb casing also depends on the way it is required to burst. Bombs used against people are designed to shatter into hundreds of fragments so that they will cause as much injury as possible. The fuses that set off the bomb must have safety devices to make sure the bombs do not go off accidentally during handling and transportation. A wire attached to the fuses activates them as they are released from the aircraft so they explode when intended.

Types of bombs

A wide variety of bombs is available to use against

185

many kinds of targets. "Armor-piercing" bombs are designed to penetrate concrete-reinforced structures and armor plate. These bombs have a high-strength steel case, a sleek body and a solid pointed nose. The shape of the body allows the bomb to reach a high speed so it will sink deep into the target. And its strength means the bomb can withstand the impact when it strikes the target. A time delay in the fusing system allows the bomb to bury itself deeply in the target before the explosive is detonated.

Depth bombs are designed for underwater destruction. Their main use is against submarines, which can be severely damaged by the pressure wave from an underwater explosion. A depth bomb has a light, cylindrical case and a flat nose to prevent it skimming across the water. A pressure-operated fuse sets off the charge when the bomb reaches the right depth. A nose fuse is also provided for use against surface targets.

Chemical bombs

All bombs contain chemicals, but the term chemical bomb usually refers to a bomb that does not rely on an explosive blast for its effect. Chemical bombs include those releasing poisonous gases, smoke and incendiary (burning) materials. Modern incendiary bombs use flammable oily mixtures, such as napalm, to destroy ground targets. Some chemical bombs are used to light up targets for observation or bombing at night.

Nuclear bombs

In the atomic bomb and hydrogen bomb, enormous amounts of energy are released from the nucleii (centers) of atoms. This is why the bombs are described as nuclear. Both types are so devastating that their power is usually equal to that of millions of tons of the explosive TNT.

Nuclear bombs explode in a brilliant, blinding flash. Heat from the flash ignites buildings and destroys life over a large area. And the tremendous shock wave that follows brings trees and buildings crashing to the ground. A further danger comes from contamination of the area by harmful radioactive dust.

See also: A-BOMBS, BALLOONS

Below: The Wheelbarrow, a remote-controlled vehicle used to investigate and move suspected explosive devices. This machine can be fitted with various devices, depending on the job it has to do. It carries a TV camera and floodlight, and can take X-ray pictures of suspicious objects.

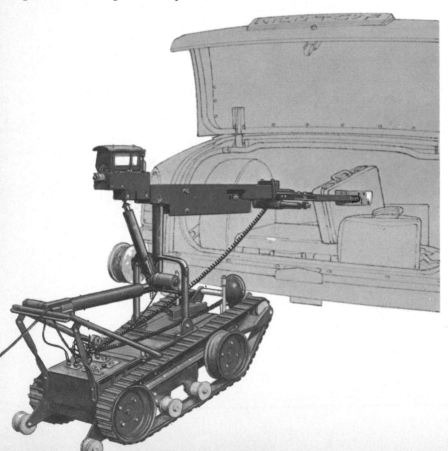
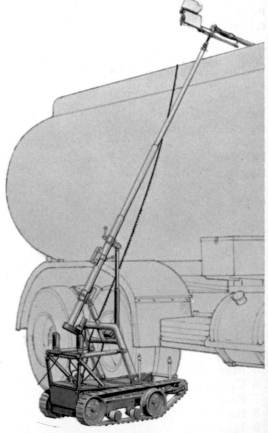

Bone Structure

The human skeleton is a marvel of design and strength. It is strong enough to protect our vital organs, is specially designed to keep the body upright, and flexible enough to allow us to move about freely.

We often see skeletons in museums. The bones are hard, brittle and dead. Bones inside us are hard too, but they are very much alive. Our bones are just like any other part of us. They have blood vessels and nerves, and if they are broken they knit together again. Bones also grow. A newborn baby is less than 2 feet (60 centimeters) long. By the time he is an adult he may be 6 feet (1.8 meters) tall. The bones will have grown three times bigger.

What are bones?

There are about 206 bones in the average adult. They have a hard outer layer and a soft middle called the MARROW. Bones are as strong and tough as concrete. They can support great weights without bending or breaking.

The bones are joined together by joints and moved by muscles which are attached at each end of the bones. The commonest disease that affects our bones is arthritis. This painful complaint causes the joints to stiffen.

The skull

The skeleton is a framework on which the other parts of the body are hung and supported. Each part of the skeleton does a particular job. The skull protects the brain, the eyes and the ears. The teeth are attached to the skull, allowing us to eat. There are holes in the skull for the eyes, the ears, the nose and the mouth. At the bottom of the skull there is another hole through which the spinal column passes. Inside this column is the spinal cord which connects the brain to every other part of the body.

Right: The skeleton protects and supports the whole body. The bones work together with the muscles to let us bend, run and jump about in an amazing way.

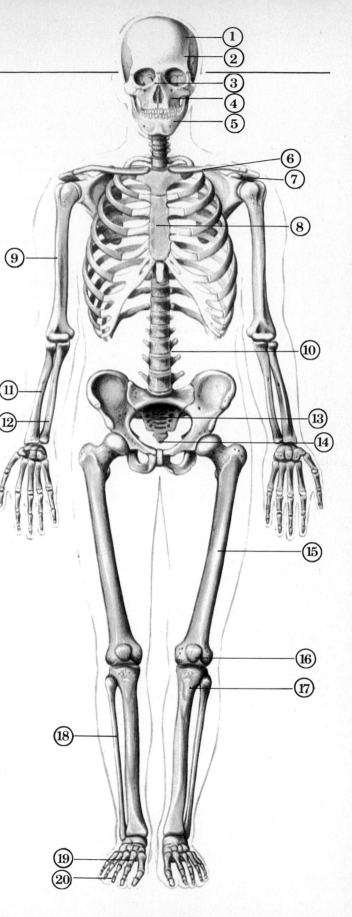

1 Cranium	11	Radius
2 Frontal bone	12	Ulna
3 Nasal bone	13	Sacrum
4 Maxilla	14	Coccyx
5 Mandible	15	Femur
6 Clavicle	16	Patella
7 Scapula	17	Tibia
8 Sternum	18	Fibula
9 Humerus	19	Tarsus
10 Lumber vertebrae	20	Metatarsus

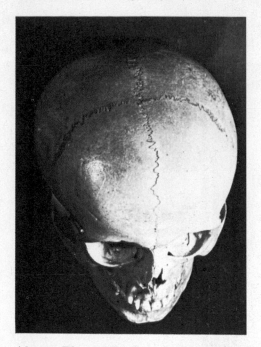

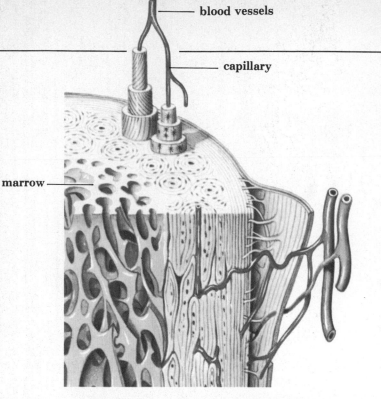

blood vessels

capillary

marrow

Above: The skull protects the brain, one of the skeleton's most important jobs. The cranium is made up of eight pieces of bone joined together. In newborn babies these bones are not joined and the joints between the bones are soft.

Above: Our bones are just like any other part of our bodies. They are full of blood vessels and nerves, running through a dense mass of bone cells. In the center of our bones is the marrow where our blood is made.

The backbone
The backbone (spine) is made up of a chain of small bones called vertebrae. Between the vertebrae are flat discs of tough cartilage or gristle. These cartilage discs act as cushions between the vertebrae. Because the backbone is made up of small bones, it can bend quite a lot. The bottom of the column is called the coccyx. In some animals the coccyx is much longer than in human beings and forms a tail.

The rib cage
The rib cage is made up of the ribs, the spinal column at the back and the breast bone (sternum) down the front. This strong cage protects the heart and lungs.

The arms and legs
The arms are joined to the spinal column by the scapula (shoulder blade) and the clavicle (collar bone). The big bone of the upper arm is called the humerus and this is joined at the elbow to the two bones of the forearm, the radius and ulna. The hand is made up of a large number of small bones. With these we can hold things and carry out delicate tasks.

The legs are attached to the spine by the pelvic girdle. The femur (the thigh bone) is the biggest bone in the body. There are two bones in the lower leg—the tibia (shin bone) and the thinner fibula. The feet, like the hands, are made up of several small bones. This lets us stand firmly and also walk and run.

Babies, men and women
A newborn baby has 350 bones, but after a while some of them grow together until it has only about 206. Its skeleton is complete by the time it is about 20 years of age. The head of a newborn baby is as long as its torso.

A woman's skeleton is smaller than a man's. It has a wider pelvis, to allow for the growing baby during pregnancy, and narrower shoulders.

The wonderful skeleton
The skeleton is truly an amazing structure. When we think about the amount of wear and tear it has to put up with during a lifetime, its strength and flexibility are quite staggering.

Broken bones
If you break a bone, this is called a fracture. Some fractures are much more serious than others because the broken bone ends can damage blood vessels and nerves. Fractures are usually treated by keeping the broken parts together inside a plaster cast. This enables the broken bones to knit back together again.

See also: BLOOD, NERVOUS SYSTEM